Edward Storrow

Protestant Missions in Pagan Lands

A manual of Missionary Facts and Principles Relating to Foreign Missions...

Edward Storrow

Protestant Missions in Pagan Lands
A manual of Missionary Facts and Principles Relating to Foreign Missions...

ISBN/EAN: 9783744756631

Printed in Europe, USA, Canada, Australia, Japan

Cover: Foto ©Lupo / pixelio.de

More available books at **www.hansebooks.com**

PROTESTANT MISSIONS

IN

PAGAN LANDS;

A MANUAL OF

MISSIONARY FACTS AND PRINCIPLES

RELATING TO

FOREIGN MISSIONS THROUGHOUT THE WORLD.

BY

REV. EDWARD STORROW,

BRIGHTON,

AUTHOR OF "INDIA AND ITS MISSIONS," "THE COMING REIGN OF CHRIST," ETC.
EDITOR OF THE "HISTORY OF PROTESTANT MISSIONS IN INDIA," ETC.

London:
JOHN SNOW & CO.
2 IVY LANE, PATERNOSTER ROW.
1888.

"It is scarcely possible to deny the extraordinary importance of the missionary efforts of our time: they are yet, in reality, in their infancy, yet it is certain that they will transform the nature and the relations of the un-christian peoples, and will thereby produce one of the most magnificent and colossal revolutions that history contains."—*Meinicke.*

"The salvation of men ought to be the aim and the desire of every Christian. The spirit of Missions is the Spirit of our Master, the very genius of His religion. A diffusive philanthropy is Christianity itself: it requires perpetual propagation to attest its genuineness."—*Livingstone.*

"The Christian Church, if true to her Divine Lord and His great commission, must be Missionary. For a Christian Church is only strong, loyal, and prosperous, as it is carried out of itself into the full unrestrained exercise of its noblest energies and completest self-denial. A Church without a deep, intense, and ever-growing missionary spirit is no real Church of Christ."—*Livingstone.*

"In the whole compass of human benevolence, there is nothing so grand, so noble, so Christian, so truly God-like, as the work of evangelising the heathen."—*William Orme.*

"It shall be my life-work to earn money to send missionaries to the heathen, reserving for myself a bare subsistence."—*Lavina Crawford.*

PREFACE.

A few lines will suffice to explain the purpose for which this book is written.

Foreign Missions are not adequately known, nor is their work rightly understood or appreciated. Even those who are familiar with the operations of one Society, usually know little of the work of others. Most professing Christians are apathetic on the subject, to a degree which, to the writer, seems sinful; whilst the irreligious regard it with an indifference, or a dislike, which is both unreasonable and unjustifiable.

It is the aim of this book, then, to present, in a condensed form, the whole subject of Christian Missions fairly before various classes of minds, with the hope that in many it may, at least, be raised to a higher and truer place.

It has been my endeavour to write from a Christian, rather than from a denominational standpoint, and impartially to include the work of all Societies and all denominations; but, in so doing, I have not thought it necessary to refrain from every expression of individual opinion.

If the reader should detect omissions or apparent errors, may I say that it will cause me regret if I have failed in any case to do justice to all true work and workers. Possibly among such a multitude of statements, all may not be found absolutely correct; yet, probably, in every instance I could give reasons for each of the statements I have made. But I trust that no errors of detail, where perfect accuracy is often so difficult, may be allowed to break the force of those great truths, principles, and facts, which, in all diffidence, I believe will be found embodied in this volume.

The two diagrams at the end of the book are inserted (slightly altered) through the kind permission of E. Stock, Esq., of the Church Missionary Society.

The Tables of the various Missionary Societies, their agents, adherents, &c., are taken, with alterations, from the *Missionary Review*, Princeton, U.S.A.

EDWARD STORROW.

BRIGHTON, *December*, 1887.

CONTENTS.

CHAPTER	PAGE
I. THE RELIGIOUS CONDITION OF THE WORLD	1
II. THE MORAL AND SOCIAL CONDITION OF NON-CHRISTIAN RACES	11
III. FALSE RELIGIONS IN THE LIGHT OF SCRIPTURE	15
IV. THE PHILOSOPHY OF MISSIONS	20
V. MISSIONARY EFFORT IN THE SIXTEENTH, SEVENTEENTH, AND EIGHTEENTH CENTURIES	28
VI. THE RISE AND DEVELOPMENT OF MODERN MISSIONS	37
VII. MISSION FIELDS AND AGENCIES—AFRICA	80
VIII. MISSION FIELDS AND AGENCIES—ASIA AND POLYNESIA	100
IX. MISSION FIELDS AND AGENCIES—AMERICA	129
X. THE RESULTS OF MISSIONS	138
XI. THE SOURCES AND CULTIVATION OF THE MISSIONARY SPIRIT	164
TABLES OF MISSIONARY SOCIETIES	178
INDEX	187

PROTESTANT MISSIONS IN PAGAN LANDS.

CHAPTER I.

THE RELIGIOUS CONDITION OF THE WORLD.

THE human race is estimated by the most competent authorities to number 1430 millions, and the forms of religion most prevalent are Christianity, Mohammedanism, Buddhism, and Hinduism. An analysis of these will show what an immense proportion of our race is without any satisfactory form of religion, and reveal clearly this principle, that under the influence of pure Scriptural Christianity mankind has reached its highest point of civilisation, power, and hopefulness; and that precisely to the degree by which Christianity is corrupted or forsaken is the civilisation lowered, the state of society more defective, and the outlook less hopeful.

The following analysis will illustrate this principle, and it could be sustained by the amplest evidence:—

Protestantism is professed by 130 millions of our race, and is the prevalent faith of England, Scotland, Holland, Prussia, Denmark, Sweden, Norway, British North America, the United States, and the Colonies of South Africa, Australia, and New Zealand. It divides with Roman Catholicism the Cantons of Switzerland and the minor States of Germany. All its oldest possessions lie, as will be observed, in regions not most favoured by nature; nevertheless these are the seats of the highest civilisation, the noblest forms of political and social life, and the most extended commerce the world has ever seen. Defects and evils there are among these States, but if their general condition be compared with that of all others, it will be seen how far they have advanced beyond them. The progress they have made in discovery, science, art, civilisation, wealth, power, freedom, during the past 150 years—since their position was fairly established—has never been attained by any other States in twice the time.

If we attempt to define what principles, institutions, and habits of life are good for individuals, for families, and for society, we find these in their highest perfection in Protestant countries. If there is hope anywhere for the world's welfare and elevation surely it is in these.

Roman Catholicism is the religion of 190 millions of our race, chiefly in France, Spain, Portugal, Italy, Austria, Belgium, Ireland, and South America. The political, social, and moral condition of these nations is lower than that of their Protestant neighbours. Their civilisation is inferior, their governments are less stable, their resources are more limited and less varied, and their progress is far slower. The two have now been side by side for 300 years, and the advance of the former over the latter in all that constitutes human progress, at the close of each fifty years, and that, too, with accelerated speed, sufficiently proves that where the pure teaching of God's Word is forsaken, the deviation brings its own curse and punishment. The poverty and factiousness of Ireland; the political unrest and social laxity of France; the manner in which Spain and Portugal, once so splendid and powerful at home and abroad, have sunk to abject weakness; and the low, unhappy condition of the South American States when contrasted with the strength, progress, and hopefulness of those in North America, clearly prove this.*

The Greek Church has 75 million adherents in Russia and Turkey; and the related *Abyssinian, Coptic, Syrian, Nestorian,* and *Armenian Churches* have about 10 millions more. The errors of these Churches are almost as great and pernicious as those of the Church of Rome. The ritual of the first-named and most important of these is imposing and gorgeous, but intensely formal and lifeless. Ignorance, superstition, and apathy prevail under all these forms of Oriental Christianity. They answer but too truly to the Saviour's description of the Church at Sardis: "I know thy works, that thou hast a name that thou livest, and art dead."

Mohammedanism has 185 million adherents. It is the dominant faith of Arabia, Persia, Turkey, the States of Central Asia, and Northern Africa; it is widely diffused throughout the other portions of Africa, and less influentially to the eastern borders of China and the southern limits of the splendid, populous, and fertile islands of the Indian Archipelago. In India alone there are 50 millions, being one-fifth of the entire population.

No Mohammedan country has ever risen above semi-barbarism. There is not one which has a form of government under which Englishmen would be satisfied to live. Nor are reforms and progress possible, without violence being done to its principles and traditions, since it petrifies whatever it touches. Its intolerance far exceeds even that of the Papacy; and, beyond ancient Mosaism, it is political as well as religious. The Koran is its statutes of the realm, as well as its theological and spiritual guide-book. Hence arises the

---

* This was conclusively proved some years ago in a book too little known, "Catholic and Protestant Nations compared in their threefold relations to Wealth, Knowledge, and Morality," by Napoleon Roussel. See also "La Question Romaine," par Edmond About.

danger and difficulty of introducing reforms into such Mohammedan countries as Turkey and Egypt. Not only does it cling with wonderful tenacity to political power, and hate and resent change and progress; it has also marvellous power to mould the disposition and character of its adherents into likeness to Mohammed himself—an evil type, the most intolerant, sensual, unamiable, and hostile to Christianity which the world anywhere presents.

Buddhism is the prevalent superstition of Ceylon, Siam, Burmah, Thibet, China, and Japan, and numbers not less than 420 million adherents. The whole of south-east Asia, with its teeming population, accepts this religion; and the history of its rise and diffusion constitutes one of the most remarkable and suggestive episodes in the religious history of mankind. In these it is in striking contrast to Mohammedanism, and in accord with the peaceful principles and most consistent incidents of Christian propagandism.

But its leading features and general influence only can now engage our attention. It has been the most powerful religious factor for more than 1200 years among gifted races, dwelling compactly in regions of the earth most favoured by nature—yet with what results? It has a certain amount of civilising, elevating power, which, however, seems incapable of expansion; for no Buddhist race has advanced beyond semi-barbarism, nor, until roused into life by contact with western civilisation, has exhibited any desire for progress for hundreds of years.

If no Buddhist race is barbarous, none is civilised. It is the vaguest and loosest of all systems of religion; for scholars have not decided whether, fundamentally, it is monotheistic or atheistic, and whether its *Nirvana* be a future conscious existence for the soul, or annihilation. Its moral teachings are singularly pure, but it has very little power over the heart and life. No religion has ever so pliantly lent itself to the idiosyncrasies of humanity, for wherever it has gone it has adopted the pre-existing superstitions, rather than subverted them,—like the ivy, taking the form of whatever it covers.*

Hinduism is the profession of 190 millions of our fellow-men, who are, for the most part, also our fellow-subjects. Of all the superstitions which have ever held sway over great masses of mankind, this is the most incongruous, strange, and tyrannical, and exercises a singular power over the imagination and the life. Intellectually, it leans toward pantheism; popularly, it is a gross system of polytheism; but transcendental monotheism, tritheism, and atheism also find in it a home. It has myriads of temples and shrines for one or other of the 335 million divinities it recognises, but only one in all the vast empire for the supreme Bramho, "the one without a second." It is without those traits of grace and beauty which characterised the superstitions of Greece and Rome; yet it treats the people of every race but its own with grotesque and supercilious contempt. The state of opinion and society it has fostered are among the most extraordinary that have ever prevailed among a numerous race. A typical Hindu supposes that his caste-rank is the consequence of something done in a previous state of existence, perhaps thousands of years ago, and that in consequence of what he does in this life he may become at death a reptile, a quadruped, or a bird. He believes that this may turn on the quality of a single meal, or the caste of the person with whom he eats, or the trade he follows, or the place where he resides. He supposes that women are intellectually and morally inferior to men, and that, therefore, very early marriages, the seclusion of

* In Thibet it takes the form of Lamaism, with a supposed incarnation of the Deity; in Japan it coalesces with Shintoism; in China, with demon and idol worship on the one hand, and rationalism and ancestral worship on the other; in Nepaul and Ceylon, with Hinduism; and in Burmah, Siam, and Annam, with the idolatries which preceded it. If, therefore, its numerical strength be closely analysed, it will be diminished by some tens of million Chinese Confucianists and Taoists, and a large, though indefinable, multitude of Japanese Shintoists.

women from general society, their inability to read or write, their absolute subjugation to their husbands, or other male relations, and the strict prohibition of widow marriage, are customs not only wise but necessary. He supposes that his destiny depends on caste laws far more than on theological belief or moral conduct; so that, whilst he will allow himself without compunction to violate almost every moral law, he will starve or die rather than eat with the man who is as superior to him socially as the earl is to the day-labourer, but who has no caste, or one lower than his own.

In addition to these great religious systems, there are about 230 million other idolaters, scattered almost exclusively throughout Asia and Africa, whose superstitions are too rude and vague to be systematised. They are all barbarians, though in various degrees of degradation and ignorance.

It is not necessary to do more than indicate the other religions of mankind however interesting they are.

Judaism, the oldest faith in the world, older even than Hinduism, is the profession of 7 millions.

Parseism, the purest and most elevated form of idolatry—if indeed it may so be called—has not a million adherents, found exclusively in Persia and on the western coast of India.

Shintoism in Japan, and *Confucianism* and *Taoism* in China, are closely associated with Buddhism, and subtract greatly, in any careful analysis, from its numerical force. The same remark holds good of Deism, which prevails so extensively in some Roman Catholic countries, and, in a strict analysis, so materially diminishes the numerical strength of the Papacy.

Comparing these religions with each other, we find the following startling and suggestive results:—

Protestantism is the profession of only 1 in 11 of our race; Romanism of 1 in $7\frac{2}{3}$; the Eastern Church of 1 in 17;

Mohammedanism of 1 in $7\frac{1}{2}$; Buddhism of 1 in $3\frac{1}{2}$; Hinduism of 1 in $7\frac{5}{6}$; other Polytheists are one in $5\frac{3}{4}$. Thus it appears that Roman Catholicism, Mohammedanism, and Hinduism, are each numerically stronger than Protestantism. Buddhism has three times as many adherents, and the unsystematised polytheisms of barbaric races almost twice as many. Buddhism numbers as many disciples as all forms of Christianity united. The latter is received by less than one-third of the human family. Thus 1035 millions of our race are without a true Revelation, ignorant of the Supreme Being and of His purpose of redemption through Christ. This heathen and Mohammedan population is forty times that of England and Wales, or twenty-nine times that of Great Britain and Ireland! If, then, we are moved to effort when we hear of a village or some district of a large town destitute of the Gospel, what should be our emotions, as we survey this inconceivably large mass of our fellow men without a true knowledge of God and of a Saviour? The highest reason for seeking their evangelisation is found in this great fact; but there are certain aspects of their state, even in this life, which prove how greatly they are in need of Christianity as a purifying and elevating power.

1st. For instance, if the state of man be carefully surveyed, this fact will be seen, Wherever there is Christianity, there is civilisation and progress; and the civilisation is high, and the progress great, in proportion to the purity of the Christianity. But beyond the bounds of Christendom we meet with no state of society that strictly can be described as civilised. And they are without it just to the extent that they deviate from the fundamental principles of the Bible.

2nd. We discover, if we carefully study history, and the mental and moral qualities of various races, that these varieties of civilisation and barbarism, of progress and of retrocession, are not the results of geographical position, of natural advantages, or of intellectual force, but mainly of religious belief. This might be proved by a great variety of facts, from which take the following:—Syria and the neighbouring regions are among the fairest and most fertile on the earth. They were once the seats of civilisation, peopled by races of great intellectual power; but for more than 1000 years, under the blighting dominion of Islam, they have made no advance. Again, the Chinese have, in some directions, great mental gifts as well as much practical skill and force of character, through which in former ages they made great progress; but it is questionable if they have made any real advance during several hundred years. The Indo-Aryan race is one of the most gifted, and, when Christianised, will probably be one of the saintliest and most illustrious; but for 3000 years it has almost been as quiescent as its supreme divinity Bramho during one of the great cycles of his imagined being.

Thus Islamism, Buddhism, Hinduism, alike prove how deadening false religion is; and, to complete the illustration, reference may be made to another capable polytheistic race. Madagascar is no sooner touched and inspired by Christianity than it wakes out of the nightmare of ages, and rapidly advances on the pathway of civilisation.

3rd. False religion not only checks the nobler aspirations of mankind, it also degrades, demoralises, and impoverishes. The least advanced Protestant race, for instance, is far higher than the most advanced pagan one. That is, the people are better housed, clothed, fed, educated, live longer and more securely, have more wealth, and are less likely to lose it by fraud, violence, or national reverse.

4th. There are operative all over heathendom, evil principles, usages, and customs, which produce a frightful amount of misery. Turn, for instance, to Central Africa. There are to be seen races, greedy, mean, and degraded to an unspeakable degree, whose pastimes are slave hunting, the burning of villages, and the slaughter of human beings. The States of Northern Africa are chiefly known to us by their despotism and piratical proclivities. They, and all other Mohammedan States, recognise slavery, polygamy, and forms of government so despotic and corrupt that no body of Englishmen could live under them. Among the States of Central Asia the bigotry and lawlessness are such that no Christian dare venture to dwell there. In India caste, female degradation, and perpetual widowhood, produce more misery year by year than slavery ever produced in the British colonies. In China infanticide is common. In all Buddhist lands human life is imperilled by great outbreaks of violence, and unnatural, as well as natural vice is common. In the Island world of Asia, theft, violence, and ignorance are almost as general as they can be, whilst infanticide, cannibalism, and human sacrifice have been customary in many parts. And through all these vast and varied regions, truthfulness, honesty, and honour are rarely to be found. Who can estimate the unhappiness and unrest which all this engenders? for the Psalmist's words are as true now as they were 2800 years ago: "Their sorrows shall be multiplied that hasten after another god."

5th. It is a striking and pathetic feature of heathenism that it is far more fruitful of evil than of good, and seems generally impotent even to encounter the abuses and evils from which its victims suffer. This arises from its very general lack of moral principle; and since its adherents are usually without moral indignation, they have little revulsion from crime, and neither motive nor courage sufficient to attack it. In England, if a great crime be perpetrated, or a great evil be brought fairly before the public view, the moral indignation is so sensitive and strong, that numbers willingly incur expense, trouble, and danger to detect the perpetrator of the former, or unite for the suppression of the latter. But it is not so in any heathen community. Thus slavery, polygamy, infanticide, suttee, perpetual widowhood, and analogous evils exist here and there as great national institutions for hundreds of years, with only a timid voice now and again lifted in protest against them. Everywhere heathenism presents a low, hopeless, and joyless level of humanity, in strong contrast to the hopeful, elevating, and beneficent qualities of evangelical Christianity. The instances in which, during the past thousand years, it has waged war on vice and crime; subverted evil, unless by the introduction of other evils; reformed and regenerated any large proportion of society; inspired men with noble and beneficent impulses; striven to mitigate the misery produced by such calamities as famine, pestilence, and war; erected hospitals for the diseased, and schools for the young; asylums and refuges for the forsaken, the unfortunate, and the helpless—have been rare indeed. The Psalmist's words have been true of almost every age since they were penned, because of reasons inherent in human nature, "The dark places of the earth are full of the habitations of cruelty."

This is a dark picture, but it is a strictly accurate one. Heathenism is of all human evils the most offensive to God, and the most injurious to mankind, and the marvel is that we can read what the Bible says about idolatry, and have a general idea of the poverty, ignorance, vice, and misery common in all heathen lands, and yet view it with such indifference!

CHAPTER II.

THE MORAL AND SOCIAL CONDITION OF NON-CHRISTIAN RACES.

HE relations of man to God are of the first importance. These must necessarily affect, fundamentally, our condition here and hereafter. And on these are based the most powerful arguments in favour of Missions to the heathen, as, indeed, in behalf of all forms of Christian evangelisation. This aspect of Missions will receive the attention it merits in the next chapter. But the influence of religious ideas and beliefs on all the conditions of human life are worthy of the closest attention, and in themselves form a powerful argument in behalf of Foreign Missions.

I. General as the terms civilisation and barbarism are, they express the conditions of human life at its two extremes with sufficient distinctness. Now, if we consider the position of races, professing various forms of religion, in relation to these two terms we find some very striking facts.

1. We find all Christian races more or less civilised, and all polytheistic races more or less barbarous.

2. We find that where the Christianity is purest, the civilisation is highest; where the polytheism is the grossest, the barbarism is the most degraded; and that to the degree Christianity leans toward polytheism, (as with Roman Catholicism) is the civilisation defective, or the polytheism toward monotheism (as with Buddhism) is the barbarism softened.

3. The practical superiority of Christianity over all other forms of belief might be shown by an analysis of the moral and social state of any number of typical countries.

The lowest Protestant State, for instance, is far higher, in all that constitutes civilisation and the hopeful features of society, than the most advanced Mohammedan or polytheistic State. That is, the people are better-housed, fed, clothed, educated, live longer and more securely, have far more of whatever makes life and society rich, desirable, and strong. If we adopt any rational principles of moral and social life, and inquire what is desirable for the general good and advancement of individuals and families, of states and nations, we find them nowhere in polytheistic, Buddhist or Mohammedan States, but we do in Christian States; and if there are great evils in the latter, it is not because of defective principles, but the lack of true and thorough application of those they already have.

II. There are always associated with false religions, defective moral principles, pernicious sentiments, manners and customs, which, if not barbarous and immoral, are degrading and injurious. All false religions are more or less defective in the following respects:—They ignore morals as an essential part of religion—this is really so with most of the rude polytheisms of Africa and Asia; or they depreciate them to a secondary or inferior position by the prominence given to ritual and ceremony—as Hinduism does; or they give them a high place in sentiment, and ignore them in practice, from various causes—as Buddhism does; or they adopt a partial code of morals, and weaken even it by false principles and sentiments—as Mohammedanism does.

Everywhere human nature, in its weakness and frailty, needs to be restrained from evil and led into goodness by prohibitions and commands claiming Divine authority. But whilst Christianity is opposed to all the evil principles and customs from which humanity suffers, and teaches nothing which in any true sense can be detrimental to individuals, to families, or states, neither the one nor the other can be affirmed of any false religion. Oppression, slavery, infanticide, the degradation of women, and polygamy, if not universal, are so general as to affect the social state of tens and even hundreds of millions, whilst falsehood, fraud, unchastity, and violence, are yet more common. The poverty, unrest, and suffering prevalent from such causes in every non-Christian country are indescribable, and constitute a most powerful reason why not only every devout Christian, but also every philanthropist, and all interested in the elevation of our race, should at least regard with favour the Missionary enterprise, the most powerful and pronounced of all attempts to deliver the vast non-Christian portion of mankind from the evils from which they have almost hopelessly suffered for numerous centuries.

The author writes this with an unusual knowledge of the principles and practical influence of the great religious systems of the East, and a desire to see and recognise whatever in them is true and good. And each of them has much that is worthy of respect. They express the emotions, and the profoundest thoughts, of some of the most devout and intellectual races, on the sublimest of all subjects. If they have been abused and perverted by fanatics, priests, and knaves, they have also been moulded by men of great genius, and not seldom of a lofty moral type; for, apart from men of Hebrew race, the entire world can produce no three moral and religious teachers comparable, for wide-spread influence and abiding power, to Sackya Muni, the Aryan Hindu; Confucius, the Chinese; and Mohammed, the Arab. If they contain much that is false and gross, they also contain the shadow of some great truths, and the substance of some others—for a religion altogether false is an impossibility. If those faiths have failed to lift men higher, or even to fulfil the promise of their youth, it must not be forgotten that but for them Asia would probably have been barbarous instead of semi-barbarous, and her nations as morally corrupt as the ancient Canaanites. Defective and pernicious as are many of the usages and customs which these religions have introduced or fostered, it should not be forgotten that kindness to the poor, obedience to parents, respect for the aged, deference to the wise, and a profoundly religious sentiment, are very general where they prevail. But their conceptions of the eternal God are most *defective*. They have no Christ, no true method of forgiving sin, nor have they the divine and spiritual agency which is essential to regenerate human nature, and enable men to overcome sin and attain to personal holiness and goodness, and to rise toward a perfect ideal of disposition, character, and life. Only true Christianity can do this, by virtue of the Divine power resident in it. It alone, therefore, has the right to be the religion of all mankind.

CHAPTER III.

FALSE RELIGIONS IN THE LIGHT OF SCRIPTURE.

N the present day the essential difference between the Christian and non-Christian religions is not so generally acknowledged as formerly it was. The prevalent habit of thought is to regard them all as comparatively good, differing only in the degree in which a Divine element pervades them. Christianity is regarded as differing from Mohammedanism, from Confucianism, and Buddhism, not in essence, but degree; better, indeed, but not greatly so—or if better for Western races, hardly as adapted to those of Western and Eastern Asia. The best features of Hinduism, on its philosophic side, are brought into prominence—its monstrosities and filthiness are ignored. Even rude and brutal polytheisms are judged leniently, if not favourably. All are regarded as suited to the genius of the races professing them, and, therefore, on the whole, as suitable to them as Christianity, or even more so. The Koran, the Vedas, the Analects of Confucius, and the Pitakas of Buddha, are held to be little inferior to the Bible. Confucius is compared to Christ as a moral teacher, and Sackya Muni, the "Light of Asia," is held to have been as pure, benevolent, unselfish, and noble as Jesus of Nazareth, "the Light of the World."

All this springs much more from a wish to discredit the Bible and Christianity, than from respect for other religions, or any real belief in their verity; but it serves the purpose of undermining Christianity under the guise of philosophic impartiality and tolerance, and of discrediting Missions as unnecessary interferences with religions which are assumed to have in them all good and necessary qualities, and which, at the utmost, we should seek to reform and develop rather than destroy.

Much might be said in proof of the fallacy of such ideas, and, indeed, needs to be said with cogency of reasoning and an amplitude of evidence, which a well-furnished Christian apologist could easily marshal, but here would hardly find fitting space or adequate expression. Our appeal now and here is to the testimony of Scripture, and whilst to all who recognise its Divine authority, a single clear declaration is conclusive, the number, variety, and continuousness of its utterances on this question should carry the most absolute weight.

It should add to the significance of the following selection of Scripture declarations to bear in mind :—

1st. That to preserve the human race from forms of heathenism, superior in rationality and influence to those now most prevalent, was the purpose of the great revelations first made to Noah and to Abraham.

2nd. That to raise a sufficient barrier against universal polytheism, and to prepare the world to receive a religion, which, in addition to having a Divine origin, is, in a special sense, sublime, holy, benevolent, and saving, as is none other, was the great purpose of God in the formation of the Hebrew State, and in the revelation given to Hebrew seers and prophets.

3rd. That the entire drift and policy of Old Testament revelation, as formed and directed by God, was a protest and a warning against false religion, whatever its name and form.

4th. That the unvarying tone of Scripture towards false

religion is pitying, contemptuous, and indignant,—never complimentary or apologetic.

5th. That the Israelites all through their history were warned against idolatry, as they were warned against nothing else, and for nothing were they so sternly and unwaveringly punished as for their lapses into it.

And, finally, that the evidently special gift of Christ and His Gospel, is a declaration of the small value of all other forms of religion, and a demand not only that it be received, to the exclusion and repudiation of all others, but spread universally.

1. God is represented in the Bible as infinitely worthy of the worship and service of every being in the universe. He has also an infinite and absolute right to such worship and service. It is not only a duty and a privilege, but an honour and a blessedness, to know and serve Him. To be ignorant of such a glorious Being, is the greatest of misfortunes, and to refuse Him befitting service, when He is known, the greatest of sins. Exod. xx. 2-5; Deut. xxx. 15-20; Ps. cxliv. 15; Isa. xl. 18-31; xlii. 8-17; xlvi. 5-13; Jer. xi. 1-8; Hosea xiii. 4; 1 Cor. viii. 4-6; x. 7, 14, 19, 20; Rev. iv. 11; see also many of the Psalms, such as the xxxiii., xlviii., xcii., xcvi., and the cxlv.

2. That all necessary truth respecting Him, His law, and His worship, might be maintained, preserved, and diffused in the world, He chose the Israelites to be His people. Gen. xii. 1-3; xvii. 1-9; Exod. xix. 3-6; Deut. xiv. 2; xxvi. 15-19; Ezek. xx. 5-12; Rom. iii. 1, 2.

3. He was their friend because they served and worshipped Him; and to the degree they served and worshipped Him. Exod. xxxiv. 6, 7; Deut. vii. 6-15; xxviii.; 2 Chron. xv. 1-7; Ps. xcv. 6-11; lxxviii. 55; lxxxi. 6-16; lxxx. 8-11.

4. Every movement toward idolatry was strictly forbidden; and when such movements were made, they were invariably followed by exhibitions of the Divine displeasure. Exod.

xx. 23; xxiii. 13; xxxii.; Lev. xix. 4; xxvi. 1; Deut. iv. 15-20; vi. 14, 15; xxxi. 15-18; Josh. xxiii. 7, 8, 16; xxiv. 14-23; Deut. xi. 16, 17; xiii.; xvii. 2-5; xxvii. 15; Judges ii. 1-5, 11-23; iii.; iv. 1-4; vi. 1-6; Ps. lxxxi. 8-14; Ps. cvi. 34-43; Ezek. v. 5-17; vi. 6, 7; viii. 5-18; xx. 15-18; Isa. xli. 21-29; Jer. ii. 26-28; xi. 12-14; vii. 17-20; Acts viii. 32-43.

5. He was the enemy of the Philistines, the Canaanites, the Egyptians, the Assyrians, Babylonians, and Persians, solely because they did not worship and serve Him nor keep His laws. Exod. xxiii. 23-25; Lev. xviii. 1-3, 24-30; Num. xxxiii. 4; Deut. xii. 2-4, 30, 31; xx. 16-18; Ps. lxxix. 6; ix. 17; Isa. ii. 8, 9, 18, 20; xix. 1-4; xlv. 14-16; Jer. iv. 1, 2, 35-40; Micah v. 11-15; Chron. xx. 5-12; Zeph. ii. 9-11, 12; Acts xvii. 16-29; Rom. i. 18-32.

6. Idolatry is always spoken of and treated as the special object of His displeasure, as a sin, or a crime, or a folly, or a misfortune, and as the sure cause of loss and suffering. Num. xxv. 1-5; Deut. vii. 1, 16, 25, 26; xxix. 16-28; 1 Kings xxi. 26; see many similar passages in Kings and Chronicles; Ps. xcvii. 7; cxv. 3-9; cxxxv. 15-18; xvi. 4; lxxiv. 20; Isa. xxxi. 6, 7; xliv. 9-20; Hab. ii. 18-20.

7. The servants of God are always urged to discountenance idolatry, and to seek its overthrow; and its abandonment is always regarded with gladness. Ex. xxxiv. 12-17; Num. xxxiii. 51. 52; Deut. vii. 1-10; Ps. ii.; lxxii.; Isa. ii.; xlix. 6-26; lx.; Jer. xvi. 19-21; Hosea xiv. 3; Dan. vii. 13, 14; Mal. i. 11.

8. In the New Testament, Christ is represented as the sole source of eternal life. Acts iv. 12; John iii. 14-17, 36; v. 24; xiv., 6; Acts iv. 12; 1 Tim. ii. 5; 1 Cor. viii. 5, 6. Those who truly believe in Him become the children of God, and will finally be saved. Ezek. xviii. 20-24; Luke xii. 47, 48; John iii. 18-21; Rom. i. 18-32; Rom. ii. 5, 16; Gal. iii. 20-22; 1 John v. 19; Rev. ix. 20, 21. Hence the

joy with which the establishment of the Gospel was welcomed. Ps. lxxii. 1-3, 7-10; Isa. ii. 2-4; xl. 1-5, 9-11; li. 3-6; Luke i. 15-17, 23-33, 46-55, 67-79; ii. 8-20, 29-32. Hence the profound emotions of the Saviour in contemplating the relations of men toward Himself. Ps. xl. 6-8; xvi. 8-11; Isa. liii. 11; Matt. xi. 25-30; John iv. 21-26; vi. 32-35, 37-40; xii. 32; xvii. 1-5, 20-26. Hence His desire that the Gospel should be everywhere proclaimed, and everywhere be received. Isa. liv.; Matt. ix. 36-39; xxviii. 18-20; Eph. iv. 8-13. Hence the zeal with which His disciples, after His ascension, went everywhere preaching the Word. Mark xvi. 15-20; Acts ii. 14; iii. 11; iv. 19; viii. 1, 4; Rom. xv. 16-23; 1 Cor. ix. 16; xii. 2; 2 Cor. ii. 14-16; 1 Thess. i. 9.

CHAPTER IV.

THE PHILOSOPHY OF MISSIONS.

HE subversion of ancient and deeply-rooted superstitions, especially of the three great systems which prevail in Asia, and hold in thrall half the human race, is an undertaking so stupendous, and involves issues so important, that it can only be justified by very powerful reasons.

Those superstitions harmonise with the idiosyncracies of great races. During more than a thousand years they have expressed the spiritual cravings of hundreds of millions of people. They have been the most powerful factors in forming their thoughts, feelings, and habits, and they prevail among the most immobile and conservative of races. To overthrow them, and put in their place a faith utterly different in principle and aim, is one of the most arduous undertakings upon which any body of men, however ardent and well equipped, can enter. It necessarily involves an immense expenditure of wealth, of life, and of consecrated energy throughout a long series of years; and, if successful, of controversy, strife, mental solicitude, personal loss and suffering, domestic alienation and social revolution, if not persecution and war. Is the attempt justifiable? It is more than justifiable.

1. God has an absolute right to the worship of every human being. His rights are beyond those of parentage, of purchase, of production, of ownership, in any of their

forms. As the Lord of the universe, the Creator and the Preserver of all, He has an absolute right to the worship and service of every individual. And this justifies the uncompromising language with which His claims are everywhere asserted in Scripture, and the scorn and contempt with which every form of idolatry is treated.

This claim is not invalidated by any speciality in the object worshipped in His place, or in the circumstances of the worshippers. Their heathenism may be a sin or a misfortune—and to the degree in which it is one or the other are they to be blamed or pitied. But, however this be, the Divine rights abide, and they should be upheld and pressed by every loyal servant of the universal King as zealously as Elijah and Elisha stood up against the heathenish practices of Ahab, Jezebel, and the people of Israel.

2. The right of the Saviour to universal homage, as Lord of all, has been superinduced on the original right of God, as the Creator and Ruler, to the worship and obedience of all He created and governs. This important principle of Christian theology is interwoven with all its facts and principles. The advent of Christ had its origin in the eternal purpose of God to save men, and spiritually to rule the world through Him. Hence the preparations that were made for His advent by the Divine prescience throughout thousands of years, and the gladness with which it was anticipated by a long line of patriarchs, prophets, and holy watchers. Hence the stir in heaven and on earth with which His advent was attended, as expressed by the angels' song, "Glory to God." Hence the manner in which, with infinite calmness and dignity, He laid the foundation of a society evidently designed for universal diffusion, and to be permanent as humanity. Hence also the striking language—grand and rational only on the hypothesis that He was sent of God to be the Saviour of the world—which He addressed to His disciples after His rejection, crucifixion, and resurrection—"All power is given

unto Me in heaven and on earth; go ye therefore, and teach all nations, baptising them in the name of the Father, and of the Son, and of the Holy Ghost: teaching them to observe all things whatsoever I have commanded you: and, lo, I am with you alway, even unto the end of the world." Matt. xxviii. 18-20.

3. The disciples thus interpreted the purposes of Christ's mission, and the meaning of His final command. They came to understand that He was the Lord and the Saviour of all; that He was the propitiation for the sins of the whole world; that He was the One through whom God would henceforth communicate His richest gifts of pardon, goodness, and eternal life to mankind; and that by virtue of this Divine function, He was exalted to the right hand of God to be "a Prince and a Saviour to give repentance to Israel and remission of sins;" "to be the head over all things, to the Church, which is His body, the fulness of Him that filleth all in all," and that "God had highly exalted Him, and given Him a name which is above every name; that at the name of Jesus every knee should bow of things in heaven, and things in earth, and things under the earth; and that every tongue should confess that Jesus Christ is Lord, to the glory of God the Father." Acts v. 13; Eph. i. 22, 23; Phil. ii. 9, 11.

4. And they acted on the belief of these great truths. "They went everywhere preaching the Word." They knew that the minds of men everywhere were pre-occupied by certain forms of religious belief or superstition, which had become strong through the convictions of the people, or their habits, or hopes or interests, operative through many ages, and that the attempt to displace the existing religions by the new faith would expose them to life-long obloquy, suffering, and danger—for the Saviour had warned them of all this;* and they knew quite sufficient alike of Jewish and Gentile human nature to be assured that since the

* Matt. x. 16-42; Luke xii. 49-53; John xv. 16; xvi. 1-4.

diffusion of the Gospel meant the subversion of any existing religion, and a complete change in the opinions and lives of its adherents, they would everywhere be hated and opposed; nevertheless they fully preached the Gospel of Christ to men of every religion, every race, and every class. In their estimation an idol was nothing more than a name; Jesus Christ was all and in all, and therefore their desire was to make Him known to the entire world.

5. Of course there was a limit to their ability to preach Christianity to all the world, though there was none to their zeal and desire. And therefore it was that they inspired their converts, and those especially who entered into the sacred office, with their own convictions; so that under their divine impulses, in spite of obloquy, danger, and all forms of opposition, the Gospel was preached before the end of the third century in almost every region of the then known world.

6. All this was done calmly, earnestly, and under a deep consciousness of duty, whilst they were quite aware of the painful issues that would arise. They knew that the Saviour had declared that He "came not to send peace on earth, but a sword," and that, as the result, the father would be divided against the son . . . "and a man's foes would be those of his own household." They knew, for He had told them, that they should be "hated of all men for His name's sake," and "persecuted from city to city." They knew that the converts they made would be exposed to loss and suffering, often even in their extremest form, and that if they succeeded, the immediate result would be such a moral, social, and national revolution in every land, as the world had never witnessed.

But "these men who turned the world upside down," never hesitated for a moment in their policy. That which two of them declared, when commanded "not to speak at all nor teach in the name of Jesus," was illustrative of the spirit which actuated them all; "Whether it be right in the sight of God to hearken unto you more than unto God, judge ye. For we cannot but speak the things which we have seen and heard." Acts iv. 19, 20.

7. Were they justified in this? The leader of them, in this great enterprise, declared that necessity was laid upon him to preach the Gospel; a necessity so strong that the Divine displeasure would fall on him, in its heaviest forms of remorse and condemnation, if he refrained from the utmost delivery of Christian truth. 1 Cor. ix. 16.

8. It is well to consider the motives which urged the disciples in a course which was so arduous, which seemed so hopeless, and which involved consequences so important and varied;—

The world generally was given to idolatry, and whether its form was Grecian or Gothic, Scandinavian or Egyptian, whether it was refined and philosophic, or barbarous and rude, it was associated with vice, cruelty, and wrong, such as Paul describes in Romans i. 18, and was thus dishonouring to God and pernicious to man.

They saw that the intellectual and moral degradation which overspread society would not be successfully encountered by any internal force; for whilst the great masses of society were too gross, degraded, and hopeless to seek after anything beyond the needs and pleasures of the passing hour, the classes who should have striven to elevate their aims and hopes—priests, philosophers, and statesmen—were contemptuous of others, hopeless of society, or eager only for the advantage of themselves and their class. The world, they saw, "by wisdom knew not God."

Nearer to themselves was Judaism, and they were not slow to recognise its Divine qualities, or the splendid influence it had exerted on the Gentile world, in leavening it with higher conceptions of religion and morality, and inspiring it with the small amount of hope it then cherished. But it had run its course; and as the brightness of the stars disappears in the splendour of the sun's light, it was to lose its glory in "the glory that surpasseth." 2 Cor. iii. 4-11.

Far beyond all conceptions of the sinfulness of heathenism, the degradation and misery of the Gentile world, and the inability of Judaism to meet the wants and aspirations of humanity, was their desire to make known to the utmost possible extent the great facts of the Saviour's history, and the saving truth of which it was the basis. Christ as a person, who was the Son of God, whose miracles awed them, whose words were supremely sweet and powerful, whose character was perfect in its moral beauty, whose death was dreadful and strange, but who had risen from the dead—Him they believed to be the Son of God and the Saviour of mankind; and that to know who He was, what He had done, and what He could do for everyone, was of the first importance to make known. Therefore, it was that they went everywhere preaching Christ and the resurrection, and practically giving effect to their mission by gathering all who believed what they said into Christian communities. They had been warned by Christ, and they found by experience, that the prosecution of their mission would involve themselves in suffering and danger, their converts in persecution, and society generally in confusion; but they did not hesitate, since they knew that nothing could be worse than the existing condition of society, that great evils can never be overthrown without social convulsion, and that the good that would ensue to individuals and to society, from the diffusion of their message, would far more than compensate for immediate loss. Therefore it was that, with unflagging zeal and a courage which never quailed, they went everywhere "preaching the Word."

9. Obedience to the Divine will and commands, sympathy with Christ, and, substantially, the same motives which impelled the apostles and primitive believers, lie at the root of the Missionary enterprise in our day.

Heathenism, whatever its name and form, is toward God an insult and a wrong, and toward man a lie, a delusion, and an injury. It robs God, it degrades and impoverishes man. And this it does wherein the highest interests and destinies of men, here and hereafter, are involved. Its loftiest ideals are most imperfect—if it denounces some evils, it breeds others, and its general fruitage is dread, degradation, ignorance, selfishness; whilst, if it declares a future, that future is vague and hopeless as that of Buddhism, or gross and sensual as that of Islam, or as degrading as the transmigration of Hinduism.

Not one heathen superstition deals adequately with the great evil afflicting our race—Sin. Their protests against it, if made at all, are vague, feeble, and misleading; their pretentions to extirpate and forgive it, are a mockery and delusion. Therefore it is that, not only what we usually call immorality and vice are wide-spread as heathenism itself, but so are their social and relative forms; for oppression, despotism, cruelty, the rule of the strong and cunning, are as wide-spread as fraud, deceit, and unchastity. And this explains the poverty, fear, degradation, which are prevalent throughout heathenism; for if righteousness exalteth a nation, not only will sin be a reproach to any people, but a degradation and a hindrance also. Hence we see, that in spite of superior advantages, arising from ancient civilisation in some cases, or race superiority, or a genial climate and a fruitful land in others, so little advance has been made from barbarism or semi-barbarism toward civilisation by any race left entirely to themselves. Where it has been made, the impelling, energising force has come from without rather than from within.

Here, then, is the warrant for Foreign Missions, their justification, and more than their justification. The heathen world has lost, somehow, the true knowledge of God. It is, therefore, as a ship without a compass, a traveller who has lost his way, a lonely child in the night, a diseased man in the hands of empirics. Its present life is unsatisfactory and degrading, its future life uncertain. The Church of God has it in its power to remedy all this. We have an adequate knowledge of God and of all saving truth, This knowledge we can impart. It is as important for all as it is for us. It can accomplish for others all, and even more than it has done for us. Loyalty, then, to God, obedience to His commands, appreciation of Christ and of the great things He has done for us and can do for others; zeal for a religion which is Divine and beneficent, and against religions which are, if not diabolical, only human; and compassion for the vast multitudes, who are wandering as sheep without a shepherd,—should all impel us to "go into all the world and preach the Gospel to every creature."*

* See "The Missionary Work of the Church," by Revs. Dr. Stowell and E. Storrow. London: J. Snow & Co. Also "The Philosophy of Missions," by Rev. T. E. Slater. London: J. Clarke & Co.

CHAPTER V.

MISSIONARY EFFORT IN THE SIXTEENTH, SEVENTEENTH, AND EIGHTEENTH CENTURIES.

HE age of Modern Missions dates from the last decade of the eighteenth century; nevertheless, far more thought and effort were previously given to the promulgation of the Gospel beyond the boundaries of Christendom than is usually supposed. Nor should it be forgotten that the Protestant Churches were not in a position to undertake distinct enterprises, whilst a work which taxed their utmost energies demanded their immediate attention. They were poor, weak, unorganised, and their very existence was threatened by a powerful, subtle, and implacable foe; nevertheless they were by no means indifferent to the wants of the heathen world, and made various efforts to meet them, though, from the circumstances of the times, they did not assume our highly-organised forms.

The following brief sketch will make this clear, and the careful reader will note that these early efforts were guided chiefly by the following considerations:—1. The importance of enlarging the boundaries of Christendom by colonisation; 2. Of sustaining the Christian character of the colonies and possessions; 3. Of instructing in Christian knowledge the heathen subjects of the colonies, and 4. Of reaching, as far as practicable, the heathen beyond those limits.

As early as 1556, a band of fourteen Huguenots left Geneva, under the auspices of Calvin and the Admiral de Coligny, "with the hope of establishing the doctrines of the Reformation in Brazil, and of introducing them among the natives." Others joined them as they passed through France, and numbers hoped to follow, that they might found in America a Christian State, free from the ills which afflicted their native land. The expedition failed through the base treachery of Vice-Admiral Villegagnon, though this did not deter Coligny from sending, six years later, a similar Protestant colony to Florida, which also failed through Spanish hostility and the prevalence of disease. In 1559, Gustavus Vasa, of Sweden, sent missionaries to convert his pagan subjects in Lapland. Schools were opened and books translated. This was followed by sustained efforts of a similar nature not only by the Sovereigns and the Diets, but the people; for in 1738, the former resolved that the whole Bible should be translated into Lappanese, and the latter contributed £60,000 for the mission, schools, and the circulation of the Scriptures.

The attempts of the Dutch to spread Christianity in their foreign possessions are worthy of honour, however mistaken their methods may have been.

Walleus, professor in the University of Leyden, was the first Protestant who trained missionaries for foreign service (in 1612). In 1639 Grotius published his celebrated work on the "Truth of the Christian Religion," to assist in the diffusion of the Gospel in pagan lands. Hoornbeck, the coadjutor of Walleus, wrote a similar treatise in 1659. Twenty-two years prior to this, John Moritz, Governor-General of the Dutch West India Company, had secured the services of eight missionaries. In Java, Formosa, and Amboyna, during the first half of the seventeenth century, the Dutch adopted systematic means to Christianise the people by dividing their possessions into districts, in each of which a minister was placed, whose duty it was to educate the young and train the adult population in Christian ways. The elasticity of belief and profession induced by Buddhism, on the one side, and the appeals made by the Dutch Government, on the other, to the lower interests of the people, drew great numbers to profess the Christian faith. In Java, for instance, the Christians were said to be more than 100,000; but their profession was a mere name, and their instructors generally mere hirelings, who took little pains to make the profession a reality, with the result that when the Christian name ceased to be a passport to privilege and profit, it was cast aside.*

It was in Ceylon that Dutch zeal was most systematic, and after a period of apparent success was seen to be an ignominious failure. Immediately after the island was wrested from the Portuguese in 1636, several ministers were sent out to establish schools and Christianise the people. Had they been men of the type of Balddeus, one of their number, Ceylon probably would now have been a Christian island. With singular zeal and considerable organising power, he established schools, gathered congregations, and really endeavoured to give the people a true conception of Christianity, not only as a belief, but a life, not only in Ceylon, but on the Malabar Coast. To him, indeed, belongs the honour of being the first in modern times to preach the pure Gospel and gather communities of Protestant Christians in India. But the labours of his coadjutors generally were associated with a singularly corrupt and misleading policy on the part of the Government, with the result that whilst one hundred years ago the native Christians were assumed to number 400,000, shortly after 1795, when the island was taken by the English and all civil disabilities were removed, more than ninety per cent. relapsed into Buddhism.†

* Brown's "History of Missions," vol. i. p. 22.
† Sir Emerson Tennant's "History of Christianity in Ceylon."

After Erasmus, no man perceived more clearly the duty of Christians to evangelise the heathen, or urged it more forcibly, than Baron Von Weltz. In 1664, he published in German two pamphlets, entitled "A Christian and legal reminder to all right-believing Christians of the Augsburg Confession regarding a special Society, through which, with the Divine help, our evangelical religion could be extended." The other an "Invitation for a Society of Jesus to promote Christianity and the Conversion of Heathendom." He urged the establishment of a Mission College in every Protestant University, and after he had been consecrated "an apostle of the heathen," took with him 36,000 marks, and went to Dutch Guiana, where he died in the cause he so nobly served.

The great Leibnitz, towards the close of the seventeenth century, proposed that German missionaries should be sent to China, by way of Russia.

Hans Egede, in 1721, left his peaceful pastorate in Norway to carry the Gospel to Greenland, where, under the pressure of extraordinary difficulties, he laboured for many years. His success was small, but the romantic features of the mission, and the personal heroism of Egede and his wife, had great influence in forming the missionary spirit which at the end of the century became so manifest.

It was, for instance, the presence of two Eskimos in Copenhagen in 1731, recently baptised by Egede, and of a negro, who described to Count Zinzendorf and his attendants the sufferings of the negroes in the West Indies, and their eagerness to receive Christian instruction, whilst there was no one willing to give it, which first kindled the missionary enthusiasm of the Moravian Church. In the following year, when their communicants did not exceed 600, most of whom were poor and distracted by persecution and exile, they sent two of their number to St. Thomas in the West Indies; in 1733, other two to Greenland; and in the nine following years, others to St. Croix, Berbice, North America, Surinam, Tartary, Lapland, the West Coast of Africa, the Cape of Good Hope, and Ceylon. The noble lead they then took has ever since been well sustained, for no Christian community, in proportion to its numbers, has sent out an equal number of missionaries. At the present time it has 323 European missionaries, and 1575 native assistants, who are labouring for the most part among the most neglected races, and in the least attractive regions of the globe.

The briefest reference only can be made to the beginning of the most stupendous task which the Church of Christ has ever undertaken. In 1704, Dr. Lütkens, one of the chaplains of Frederic IV. of Denmark, suggested to his Majesty the duty of seeking the conversion of the Hindus in his possessions, on the south-east coast of India. Through Francke of Halle, Bartholomew Ziegenbalg and Henry Plutscho were selected for this important undertaking. They justified the wisdom of the choice by high consecration, indomitable energy, and great sagacity. Soon after they reached Tranquebar, on 9th July 1706, they set about the acquisition of the Tamil tongue, preached at once to their countrymen, and in a short time to the natives; established schools, translated portions of the Scriptures into Tamil; baptised five adult heathens on 12th May 1707, opened their first native church, and baptised more converts in the following August and September; and completed the first translation of the New Testament into an Indian language on 21st March 1711. Subsequently Grundler in Madras, Schwartz in Tanjore and Trinchinopoly, Jaenicke in Tinnevelly, and a few others, sustained and extended the work thus nobly begun. Nevertheless the missions languished toward the end of the century. Patronage and support failed from Denmark. The native churches were left without pastors, or in the hands of men not remarkable for their zeal. Preaching to the heathen was neglected; and the early missionaries had strangely neglected to train their best converts to preside over churches, or to preach to the heathen. The work, therefore, so splendidly begun, languished, and it was not until the English Societies had well entered on their work, early in the present century, that the fair promise of the early days was recovered.*

We now turn to the part taken by our own countrymen in this enterprise. It had a far larger share of their thoughts, and entered more into their purposes than is usually supposed, and our regret is that the ample evidence we have collected in proof of this can only be glanced at.

Even as early as the reigns of Elizabeth and James I., zeal for conquest, discovery and colonisation was frequently associated with a strong desire to extend the kingdom of God.

For instance, in 1589, Sir Walter Raleigh gave the sum of £100 "in especial regard and zeal of planting the Christian religion in those dark countries" of America.

Heriot, the friend and secretary of Raleigh, says that "many times and in every town, according as he was able, he made a declaration of the contents of the Bible to the people."

In the letters patent granted by James I. in 1606 for the plantation of Virginia, it is said, "So noble a work may by the providence of God, tend to the glory of His Divine Majesty, in propagating the Christian religion to such people as yet live in darkness and miserable ignorance of the true knowledge and worship of God."

Three years afterward a new charter was granted, and a few months before the expedition sailed, William Crashaw, preacher at the Temple, in a noble sermon said, among other things, to the Virginian Council, "Remember, the end of this voyage is the destruction of the devil's kingdom, and the propagation of the Gospel." Turning to Lord De La Warr, the captain-general of the expedition, and his subordinates,

* "History of Protestant Missions in India," by Revs. M. A. Sherring and E. Storrow. Religious Tract Society.

he said, "Look not at the gain, the wealth, the honour, the advancement of thy house; but look at those high and better ends, that concern the kingdom of God. Remember thou art a general of Christian men, therefore, principally look to religion. You go to commend it toward the heathen, then practise it yourselves." One of the first things done in the colony was the erection of a college at Henrico, "for the training and educating the children of the natives in the knowledge of the true God." Letters were written by James and the two Archbishops, inviting the members of the Church throughout the kingdom, to contribute "as well for the enlarging of our dominions, as for the propagation of the Gospel among the infidels, wherein there is good progress made." This was the first general collection made for missions in England, and the people generously responded by contributing the large sum of £4000.

Charles I., when granting a charter to colonise Massachusetts in 1628, expressed the wish that the colonists might be "so religiously governed as their good life may win and incite the natives of the country to the knowledge and obedience of the only true God and Saviour of mankind." And his Puritan subjects in this respect, at least, sympathised with his Majesty. One of the Pilgrim Fathers was set apart "to promote the conversion of the Indians," and subsequently they legislated in 1636 for the preaching of the Gospel among them. But John Eliot was the first missionary to the heathen in America, in the true sense. For fifty-eight years he laboured for the conversion of the Indians, and had the joy of baptising the first converts, founding the first Church, gathering the first communicants, training the first native preachers, and translating the Bible into an Indian tongue. Yet greater results followed in the influence he exerted on others to follow a like cause. The Mayhew family and David Brainerd are the best known of his successors, but his influence affected many others, and indeed it powerfully affects the missionary ardour of the American Christians to the present time. The impulse, indeed, which led to Eliot's self-sacrificing labours, produced the first missionary society ever formed in England. During Cromwell's protectorate an ordinance was passed in 1649, authorising the formation of a corporation to be called "A Society for the Propagation of the Gospel in New England," and a collection was ordered to be made in its behalf in all the parish churches of England and Wales. This charter was renewed at the Restoration, and enlarged so as to include "the parts in America adjacent to New England." Eliot received for some years substantial aid from its funds, and so did several other missionaries to the Indians.

We have clear, ample, and most interesting proof that Robert Boyle, Dr. Edward Pocock, Dean Prideaux, Bishop Berkeley, Dr. Doddridge, and others, not only thought of the conversion of the heathen, but in some instances consecrated great wealth and learning, and much time, to practical effort in this direction.

But more than a passing notice must be given to the formation of two great Societies, which, all throughout the eighteenth century, nurtured the growing missionary spirit, sustained many of the individual efforts already alluded to, and ministered largely to the Christian wants of our possessions and colonies alike in America, Africa, and Asia.

The zeal and wisdom of Dr. Thomas Bray, the ecclesiastical commissioner of Maryland, led to the formation, in 1698, of "The Society for Promoting Christian Knowledge." This was at once so successful that, with the powerful aid of Archbishop Tenison, and Compton, Bishop of London, he obtained, in 1701, a Charter for "The Society for the Propagation of the Gospel in Foreign Parts." These two Societies, whilst closely identified with the Church of England, and mainly associated with Christian effort for the conversion of Roman Catholics and the maintenance of

Christian truth in our Colonies and dependencies, have been ever mindful of the heathen, and, in their earlier days, gave noble and most timely aid to many labourers outside the pale of the Episcopal Church of England. The former Society in various ways assisted, almost from the beginning, and well on throughout the century, the Danish and German Missionaries of Southern India, and most of those Missions finally came into the hands of the younger Society. Had it not been, indeed, for British succour, the Missions would have been far weaker than they were, and probably would, in most instances, have died out.

The history thus briefly given is quite sufficient to prove that the early Protestant Christians were by no means without zeal for the propagation of the Gospel, as soon as ever they were free from the death struggle with the Papacy. But this sketch is illustrative rather than exhaustive, and it would have been a true joy to the writer to have made it the latter rather than the former, not only as the record of very noble Christian deeds and aspirations, but as a contribution to the true history of Christian Missions; for in our complacency, on account of the splendid growth and diffusion of Foreign Missions during the present century, we are apt either to ignore or despise the kindred work previously attempted, often under difficulties to which we are strangers, and with an unselfishness, endurance, and heroism we may well desire to inherit.*

---

* I am indebted, though by no means entirely, for the information here embodied to the following authorities:—Brown's "History of Christian Missions," 3 vols.; "The History of the Church of England in the Colonies and Foreign Dependencies of the British Empire," by the Rev. J. M. Anderson, M.A., 3 vols.; "Missions of the Church of England," by Ernest Hawkins; "A Short History of Missions," chapters x. xi. xii., by George Smith, LL.D.

CHAPTER VI.

THE RISE AND DEVELOPMENT OF MODERN MISSIONS.

It is not necessary to describe minutely the causes which have led to such a manifestation of missionary zeal on the part of all strong Protestant Churches as we now witness. They have been various. Protestants, as already stated, having freed themselves from the death grip of the Papacy, were now more at liberty to look round and attend to others. Commerce and colonisation brought them into closer intercourse with various races, and elicited a wider sympathy. Increased knowledge of other countries revealed the errors of the various forms of heathenism, and the vice and degradation generally associated with them. Truer and nobler conceptions of Christianity, and a wider diffusion of its essential spirit, led to its being regarded less as a belief or a theology, and more as a practical life of holiness, benevolence, and blessedness, designed by the good God for all men, and which all therefore should be invited to share. The facts stated in the previous chapter make it clear that the missionary spirit had been growing all through the seventeenth and eighteenth centuries. It is an error, as well as an injustice to the past, to think that missions date from the close of last century. That which we are about to describe was as closely related to the past as the flower is to the bud, as the fruit is to the blossom, as the wave is to the tide.

It is also of some importance to bear in mind that the spirit and principles which gave birth within a third of a century to our principal missionary societies, are inherent in vital Christianity. They are distinctly traceable in all Old Testament foreshadowings of the kingdom of Christ; in the life and words of the Lord Jesus; in the writings and aims of the Apostle Paul; in the history of the Church during the first three centuries; and at every era since, when she has been true to her King, her principles, and her traditions. But few in any age have adequately caught the missionary spirit, and whilst recording its manifestation in later times, it is important to bear in mind that the zeal, disinterestedness, and largeness of aim which gave birth to these enterprises were then, as now, the honourable possession of a few in each Church, rather than the characteristics of all.

The Baptist Missionary Society has the honour of being the first of these Societies. Its early history illustrates the truth of the observations just made. Famed as Carey, Marshman, Ward, and Fuller became, they seemed most unlikely to make any movement popular and illustrious. The difficulties with which they had to contend, both at home and abroad, were enormous. The first collection made at the formation of the Society in 1792 amounted to only £13, 2s. 6d., and for some years after Thomas and Carey landed in Calcutta, in 1793, the income of the Society was less than £2000 annually, and its staff of missionaries less than eight.* Its distinguished history in Eastern India, in Jamaica, and in the West Indies, are well known. Its course during recent years has been marked by enterprise, judgment, and a steady growth of resources and agents.

Its most important spheres, next to those already mentioned, are in China, and on the Congo; but its agents are found also in Ceylon, Japan, Palestine, Norway, Brittany, and Italy.

---

* "Life and Times of Carey, Marshman, and Ward," by J. C. Marshman.

In these various spheres it has 438 stations, 133 missionaries, and 45,159 church members, representing a much larger number of nominally Christian people.

To this followed *The London Missionary Society*, in 1795. Since it rested on a more Catholic basis than the Baptist Society, it appealed to a much larger constituency. Its declared purpose was "to maintain at least twenty or thirty missionaries among the heathen," and its fundamental principle is thus defined:—

"As the union of Christians of various denominations in carrying on this great work is a most desirable object, so, to prevent, if possible, any cause of future dissension, it is declared to be a fundamental principle of The Missionary Society, that its design is not to send Presbyterianism, Independency, Episcopacy, or any other form of Church Order and Government (about which there may be difference of opinion among serious persons), but the glorious Gospel of the blessed God, to the heathen; and that it shall be left (as it ought to be left) to the minds of the persons whom God may call into the fellowship of his Son from among them, to assume for themselves such form of Church Government as to them shall appear most agreeable to the Word of God."

Congregationalists, Episcopalians, and Presbyterians cordially united on this basis, and the Society remains true to its unsectarian principle, though now left chiefly to the support and management of Congregationalists. Its first band of missionaries, thirty in number, of whom but four were ordained ministers, left England in 1796 for the South Sea Islands. Early in the following year they reached Tahiti, where King Pomare favourably received nineteen of them; ten others were placed on the Tonga Islands, and one at the Marquesas. Such was the enthusiasm evoked by the expedition and the tidings brought home by the captain of the *Duff* of the prospects of the missions, that the same vessel was despatched in 1798 with an equally large number of missionaries to the same group of islands, and a third expedition in 1800 consisting of twelve more. But disaster and disappointment came. The *Duff*, on her second voyage, was captured by a French privateer, and after much hardship, all the missionaries returned to England. The first and third bands of missionaries met with difficulties in Polynesia with which they were not competent to deal, and after twelve years of alternate hope and disaster it seemed as if the field must be abandoned. Then the tide turned, and though not without reverses, there have come, through this and other Societies, the splendid results which hundreds of Polynesian islands now exhibit.

Although the Society soon—too soon—withdrew from Tonga and the Marquesas, it established missions, which still exist and prosper, on the Society Islands, in 1812; the Austral group, in 1816; the Harvey Islands, in 1822; Samoa in 1836; the Loyalty Islands, in 1841; the Ellice and Gilbert Islands, in 1861, and the great island of New Guinea, in 1871.

As early as December, 1798, the Society sent the celebrated Dr. Vanderkemp, with three coadjutors, to South Africa, and has since extended its spheres throughout Kaffraria, Bechuanaland, and yet farther north. India became its third great sphere in 1804. Two of its agents then landed at Tranquebar. Madras became a station in the following year; Calcutta in 1817; and now with sixty missionaries—the third of its strength—it occupies twenty-four important stations, extending from Travancore, in the south, to Almorah, in the Himalaya. One missionary was sent to Demerara, in British Guiana, in 1807, and others subsequently to Jamaica. This Society has the honour of having sent the first Protestant missionary to China in 1807, who translated the Bible into Chinese, and now it has twenty-seven male and eight female missionaries in eight centres as important as Peking, Canton, Shanghai, and Hankow. It claimed Madagascar for Christ in 1816, and New Guinea in 1871, and sent its first missionaries to Central Africa in 1877. It has been honoured by having had an unusual number of eminent missionaries. It has now a larger staff of efficient native ministers and evangelists, and a greater number of native church members and communicants, notwithstanding the strict principles on which its churches usually are formed, than almost any other Society.

The Edinburgh Missionary Society, subsequently called the Scottish Missionary Society, was formed in 1796 by adherents of the Established and Secession Churches. Its two first missionaries were sent to the West Coast of Africa. Immediately after, a mission was commenced among the Tartars living between the Black and Caspian Seas, and after the failure of both these, it sent its agents, in 1822, to Western India. In 1824 it commenced a mission in Jamaica. Subsequently the Society ceased to exist, and the missions passed into the hands of the Church of Scotland and the United Presbyterian Church.

The Glasgow Missionary Society was established at the same time, and on the same basis as the Edinburgh Society. Its first efforts in Sierra Leone were failures, but in 1821 it commenced a mission in Kaffraria, which greatly prospered, and finally passed in 1844-47 into the hands of the Free and United Presbyterian Churches.

The Church Missionary Society was founded in 1799, under "the name of The Society for Missions in Africa and the East." Its thoroughly evangelical character, the wisdom and disinterestedness with which its affairs have usually been administered, and the large and influential constituency to which it appeals, have raised it to the noble position of having the largest income, the greatest number of missionaries, and the most extended and varied field of labour in the pagan world of any Society. Beginning with an income of only £911, and one station in West Africa, it has come to have an income of £234,600, and mission stations in almost all the great countries of heathenism. Its most successful spheres are West Africa and South India, but, perhaps, in the thoughts of God, the toil it expends in the hard and less productive fields of British North America, Persia, and Eastern Equatorial Africa, may be of as much value.

The Religious Tract Society, was also founded in 1799. Although not a distinctly missionary society, it is so sympathetic with missions, and aids them so efficiently and liberally, that its services are simply inestimable. Its Missionary Fund, last year, amounted to about £28,000, and its missionary expenditure to £47,000, and by far the greater number of the 172 languages in which its publications are issued are spoken by non-Christian races.

These remarks are also applicable to *The British and Foreign Bible Society*, founded in 1804; *The National Bible Society of Scotland*, formed in 1860 by the fusion of three kindred societies; and *The Christian Vernacular Educational Society for India*, formed in 1858. The first mentioned has all through its noble history rendered to foreign missions inestimable service, for it has aided in every way to translate and print the Scriptures into new languages and dialects, and to circulate them with a wise yet liberal hand. Of the 255 languages and dialects in which directly and indirectly, it prints and circulates the Scriptures, a large proportion are spoken by heathens and Mohammedans.

The Wesleyan Missionary Society was formed in 1814, although, from the days of Wesley, Methodists had sought the conversion of the heathen almost as eagerly as of British settlers and colonists. The Society is more than an agency to reach non-Christian races. It has missions in several British colonies, and in seven European kingdoms. Those that come under our survey are in four important districts in Ceylon, South and North-East India, two Chinese centres, several parts of South and East Africa, Honduras and the Bahamas in the West Indies; and now stations are projected in Upper Burmah.

Besides those, the *Australian Methodists* have become

sufficiently self-reliant to take charge of important spheres, some of which, as the Fiji and Tonga islands, have yielded remarkable results.

The Church of Scotland assumed, after much hesitation, a definite missionary attitude toward the close of the first quarter of the present century, although missionaries had been sent, as we have seen, by two Scottish Societies as early as 1796 to West Africa; to Tartary in 1802; to Kaffraria in 1821; to Bombay in 1822; and to Jamaica in 1824. Several of the most eminent of the early missionaries of the London Society were Scotch Presbyterians. In the latter year the Church itself avowed its missionary character, and, after quite sufficient deliberation, sent her first and greatest missionary, Alexander Duff, to Calcutta in May 1830. Perhaps no missionary of the present century comes up to his level of greatness, although many have excelled him in single qualities. His life marks a new era in Scottish missionary history, in the policy of Indian missions, and in the elevation of the missionary spirit through all the Churches of Great Britain, Ireland, and America. The Scottish Church, five years afterwards, adopted Bombay and Poona as additional spheres, and subsequently Madras and Nagpur. At the Disruption, in 1843, all the missionaries joined the Free Church, whilst the buildings remained the property of the original mission; but Calcutta, Madras, and Bombay have continued stations of the Established Church. In 1856 it entered the Punjab, where it now has four important stations. Darjeeling was its next acquisition in 1870; and three years later it occupied another station, Kalimpong, in the same region. Blantyre, in East Africa, was begun in 1874; Domasi, ten years later; Ichang, in China, in 1872; and last of all, a mission in Independent Sikhim, supported from the four Scotch Universities, was founded in 1886.

In 1843 *The Free Church* began its fine missionary

career. The Church of Scotland missionaries then in India were of unusual ability, and, since the whole fourteen transferred their services to the Free Church, it commenced its missions under very favourable auspices. Since then, whilst retaining its important educational agencies in Calcutta, Bombay, Poona, Nagpur, and Madras, and extending them to reach the women of India, and the masses by evangelistic effort, it extended its energies to South Kaffraria, in 1844, where it has founded the fine industrial and evangelistic Lovedale Institution; to North Kaffraria, in 1868; Zululand, in 1867; Livingstonia, on Lake Nyassa, in 1875. It has given important aid to the New Hebrides Mission since 1876; and has valuable school and Medical agencies in the Lebanon. Its last undertaking, though deeply interesting, is in an untried and unpromising field. It assisted the Honourable T. N. Keith Falconer, in 1887, to begin a mission among the Arabs near Aden. The rank, the scholarly reputation, and the unselfish zeal of the founder, and the medical skill of Dr. Stewart Cowen, promised to give it a status which a purely evangelistic mission amongst an intolerant race would not have gained; but the early hope has been clouded by the death of the founder. His family, with the guidance and aid of the Free Church, purpose to prosecute the mission by the services of two agents.

The Free Church missions are ably conducted both at home and abroad. The great educational excellencies for which they became famous have not passed away. Nevertheless, to those have been added evangelistic, medical, industrial, and female departments of great efficiency. Its resources have grown in a very satisfactory manner. From a total of £42,775 in 1878-9, they have advanced to £81,538 in 1886-7, more than £23,000 of which is given abroad, chiefly the product of grants in aid of school and college fees.

The United Presbyterian Church assumed a definitely

missionary policy in 1835, when it took charge of some missions in the West Indies, where one-third of its missionaries and more than half its native communicants are now found. Next to this, Rajputana has the greatest number of its missionaries. There, at ten stations, some of them as important as Jeypore and Oodeypore, it labours almost alone among 12 millions of one of the most capable and interesting of the Indian nationalities. Its five European medical missionaries, who, last year, administered no less than 184,000 times to the wants of the sick, its ten Zenana lady visitors, and its 5000 scholars attest there to the extent of its work. Next to this, is its wide Kaffrarian sphere. Then that in China, which recently has transferred some of its power to vast, little known, and less cared for, Manchuria. Japan, Old Calabar, and Spain, complete its spheres. The missions generally are well conducted, have varied and efficient agencies, and are progressive.

The Presbyterian Church of England sent out its first missionary to China in 1847, and wisely concentrates its energies on that splendid sphere, where at Amoy, Swatow, and Formosa it has met with considerable success. It has also one missionary at Singapore, and one at Rampore Bauleah, in Central Bengal.

The Welsh Calvinistic Methodists wisely confine their foreign Mission, formed in 1840, to one sphere (as all small Societies should), and occupy the interesting provinces of Assam and Cachar in North-East India.

The Irish Presbyterians have had a small number of agents in Guzerat since 1840, and since then have established yet smaller missions in China and Syria.

Turning back from this convenient grouping of the Presbyterian Missions, we observe that the *General Baptists* founded their Society in 1816, and sent their first missionary to Orissa. Here, and in the adjoining districts of Ganjam and Sambalpur, they have ever since steadily laboured, and with a fair amount of success. The mission, though chiefly evangelistic, is sufficiently varied and complete. Several of its converts have been able preachers, who have had a remarkable history. Its 12 stations, with their branches, are well placed, and economically worked by 8 missionaries, 9 ladies, and 23 native preachers. Through their exertions in frequent preaching journeys, and at the great annual Juggernaut festivals, as well as by constant preaching in their principal stations, a knowledge of Christian truth has been widely spread.

The Society for the Propagation of the Gospel, whilst helpful to missions to the heathen all through the previous century, did not adopt a distinctly foreign missionary policy until 1821. Its efforts are largely directed to British possessions and colonies, and its policy is to spread in them, and beyond, Anglican Episcopalism, by the formation of dioceses and the multiplication of bishops. In these directions it has been very successful.

Its spheres in pagan lands are also numerous, including Japan, China, South-East Africa, Madagascar, British North America, and some smaller fields. In India, its agencies are alike numerous and wide-spread, and in its south-east corner it can boast of no fewer than 44,000 converts.

Here our survey of the rise and history of British Societies must cease. This is a sketch, and not a history. We must reserve space for a more extended survey of American and Continental Societies, since they are less known in England. But before turning to them, it may be remarked—

1st. That the formation of Societies similar to those already described, has continued up to the present time, and has assumed, not only great strength, but new and interesting features.

2nd. All the Societies we have mentioned continue, or have developed into others of greater strength and stability, and each one has now far greater resources than their most sanguine friends at the outset ventured to anticipate.

3rd. Less powerful denominations, such as *The Society of Friends, The Countess of Huntingdon's Connexion,* and the smaller *Methodist bodies,* have now their foreign missions.

4th. *The Churches in the Colonies* of Australia, New Zealand, South Africa, and Canada, have their missions, not only for the heathen at their doors, but in far off lands. Thus missionaries from Canada labour in India and the New Hebrides, whilst the Wesleyans of Australia have assumed charge of the missions in Tonga, Samoa, New Britain, and New Ireland.

5th. *Women's Missions,* either as independent organisations, or as auxiliaries to the older societies, have, during the last third of the century, greatly multiplied. In India especially has their agency a vast, an important, and a unique field. There the condition of women is more degraded and deplorable than it is anywhere else, not even excepting the regions blighted by Mohammedanism. There only can women reach women. And now, after weary waiting, through the presence and example of Europeans, and the powerful influence of education, all questions relating to the position of women are coming to the front, and are affording wide though peculiar openings to ladies who combine missionary zeal with medical, surgical, and educational skill.

6th. *Medical Missions,* on similar basis, have also become numerous. In the middle of the century there were not 20 medical missionaries—now they number 170—and women, as well as men, are being trained for the medical profession.

For some years the *Edinburgh Medical Missionary Society* has been training agents for this important service; and in the *Zenana Medical College, London,* during the past six years, 70 women have received a large amount of training, and are now doing excellent service in various foreign fields.

Also, since 1885, there has been a Training College at Chicago, which appears likely to become a distinct and independent missionary agency.

Though not distinctly missionary, the *Female Medical Association*, established by Lady Dufferin in India last year, is more than worthy of notice. By training English and native women as doctors, surgeons, midwives, and nurses, and encouraging their employment in native families, immense evils will be alleviated, and great positive good produced. The excellence of its aims, as well as the prestige of the Governor-General's wife, have secured as its income for the first year the large sum of £23,000.

7th. It is one of the healthiest and most hopeful signs that many mission churches are not only growing into strength and independence, but are becoming centres of evangelistic energy. Many mission stations have grown into self-supporting churches—others are growing towards independence. Converts, in growing numbers, not only become ministers and evangelists, but missionaries to foreign lands, and the Christian communities are, in some instances, sufficiently strong and zealous to begin missions on their own account. The splendid sums regularly contributed by Polynesians to the London and Wesleyan Societies; the continuous stream of Polynesian evangelists sent to the Caroline and Marshall islands, and especially to New Guinea; and the home missions established by the converts in Burmah, Madagascar, and Santalisthan, are evidences of this.

8th. In recent years new departures in missionary enterprise have become common. They are so varied and individualised that it is difficult to group them. The term independent, perhaps, is that which forms their most general characteristic. They have had their origin in individual zeal and devotedness. They appeal to personal rather than to denominational sympathy and liberality. They aim, in some instances, to be self-supporting. Their course may well be watched with great interest and some solicitude. The sphere of foreign missions is so vast and varied that it offers ample scope for any possible number of true workers; and the success of past and present agencies has not been, in all instances, so marked as to preclude the conception of something more effective. But the old Societies have been nurtured and managed with such a consensus of holy purpose, prayer, and wisdom, and they have done their work so well, that grave responsibility rests on those who, by establishing other agencies, withdraw from them sympathy and support. This, too, is obvious; those who think they discern, in their new methods of action, "more excellent ways" of spreading Christian truth, should suspend alike their depreciation of the methods of others, and confidence in the efficacy of their own, until they have stood the test and strain of one or two decades, or produced results which others cannot show.

One of the first, and perhaps the most important of this group of independent Missionary Societies, is the *China Inland Mission*. This Society was formed in 1865 by Mr. Hudson Taylor, after, at least, six years of careful preparation, and it has gradually extended its itinerating missionary agency to most of the inland provinces of that vast empire.

With an income of about £25,000, it has in China about 190 men and women workers, and is now asking for 100 more, and an increase to its resources of £12,000 or £15,000 annually. Faith is the leading principle on which its directors, and those it sends out, profess to act. No one receives a fixed salary, and some take no pecuniary aid.

Mr. and Mrs. Grattan Guinness have recently done much to create an interest in missions, to widen their sphere, and to send out a great variety of agents. Their *Missionary Institute at Bow*, trains women as well as men, for pagan

E

as for other spheres. The Livingstone (Congo) Mission was nurtured into strength under their influence.

Bishop Taylor's Missions, in India and Central Africa, and the *Salvation Army Agencies*, in South and West India, are the most recent and noticeable of these new movements.

AMERICA.

The missionary spirit created and perpetuated by men of the Puritan type like Eliot, Brainerd, and the early Moravians and Methodists, expressed itself in attempts to convert the Indians of the West and North, and the Negroes of the South, and was not slow to crystallise into the society form after the example set by earnest English Christians.

The first society formed was *The American Board of Commissioners for Foreign Missions*, in 1810. Like the London Missionary Society, it was founded on a non-denominational basis, but was mainly supported by Presbyterians and Congregationalists. It has had a noble history. It is now practically a Congregational Institution.

The first three agents were sent to Calcutta in 1812. After much opposition from the Indian Government, two of them eventually settled at Bombay, where the Society yet labours. In 1831 it commenced in Ahmednuggur among the Mahrattas, and subsequently in the districts of Sholapur and Satara; then in 1834, in the interesting province of Madura, where at eleven stations thirteen missionaries cultivate a wide and varied field.

Turning to the early history of the Society, it began in 1816, in Ceylon; in 1817, among the North American Indians; and in 1819, adopted Turkey as a sphere. Here, especially in the European provinces of the empire, it has a larger staff of missionaries than any other society; but the difficulty of even touching the Mohammedans, constrains its efforts to be mainly directed toward the education of the lapsed

Christian races. Its fine schools, with their 15,000 pupils, are of great and general use, and its literary agencies reach classes which the missionary can reach in no other way.

Its next field was the Sandwich Islands, to which it was led in a singular manner, and where, a few years after it was occupied in 1820, some of the most striking results of modern missions were won. A Sandwich Island youth, named Obookiah, found his way to New Haven, in Connecticut. The college buildings there attracted his attention, and, learning their use, he was found one day weeping at the door because he could not be instructed. This led, in 1816, to the formation of a mission seminary under the auspices of the Board, the aim of it being thus defined:—"The education in our country of heathen youths, in such manner as, with subsequent professional instruction, will qualify them to become useful missionaries, surgeons, physicians, schoolmasters, or interpreters; and to communicate to the heathen nations, such knowledge in agriculture and the arts as may prove the means of promoting Christianity and civilisation." The seminary opened with 12 pupils, of whom 7 were from the Sandwich Islands. But the varied characters of those subsequently received may be inferred from those there in 1823, when 9 were Sandwich Islanders, 15 North American Indians from seven different tribes, 3 Chinese, 2 Greeks, 1 New Zealander, 1 Malay, 1 Portuguese, 1 Jew, and 3 Anglo-Americans.

Out of the Sandwich Island Mission sprang, in 1852, that to Micronesia. The Zulu Mission of the Board was commenced in 1835. It was the first Protestant Society which, in 1837, attempted to enter Japan, though it was thwarted until 1869. Its large missions in the north of China date only from 1854, although early in the century it attempted to found a mission there. Its West-Central African sphere was adopted in 1820, and that in Central Africa as recently as 1883. It has also, since 1872, directed its energies to the Catholic populations of Austria, Spain, and Mexico. Its general features may be thus summarised for 1886 :—

Stations and out-stations	904
Ordained and lay missionaries	173
Women agents	261
Ordained native ministers	151
Native catechists	412
Schoolmasters and other helpers	1,401
Communicants	26,129
Income	£131,565

Of the income, £29,020 came from Women's Boards, which in America are far more numerous and active in raising funds and sending out agents, than similar organisations in England.

The Baptist Missionary Union was next formed in 1814. Burmah was its first and yet remains its principal sphere. In 1840 it commenced a small mission among the Telugus of South-Eastern India, which, after a long night of watching and waiting, has recently met with extraordinary success. In 1841 it began in Assam, and since then has formed missions in China, Japan, and Liberia. In 1885 it took charge of the Livingstone Congo Mission, which had outgrown the resources of its English founders. Some features of the Union are noticeable. Like some American Societies, and unlike our European ones, it appears to have more female than male missionaries.* The former number 130, the latter 96. The ordained native missionaries are 193; unordained 1024. Its communicants are 56,439.

---

* This arises from the usage adopted by many American Societies of thus classing all the wives of missionaries, as well as those specially sent out to distant spheres of labours. The usage is misleading. Only the latter class should thus be named.

Of its 588 churches in Asia as many as 325 are self-supporting; but, very wisely for its own sake and theirs, it does not sever its connexion with them. Of its income of £76,990 for 1886, £16,630 came from three women's societies.

The Baptists have also the following smaller foreign missionary societies:—

The Free Will Baptists since 1836 have been in the north of Orissa, having their English co-religionists to the south. The mission is conducted by 5 male and 14 female agents from America. It has been efficiently conducted all along.

The Southern Baptist Convention separated in 1845 from the Missionary Union on the slavery question, and has now 45 American agents in Africa, China, Italy, Mexico, and Brazil.

The Seventh Day Baptists have had, since 1847, a small mission in China.

The Canadian Baptists formed a Society in 1866, and have now 4 missionaries at 3 stations in Telingana, India.

The Disciples of Christ have 22 male and 18 female missionaries in Jamaica, Turkey, India, China, Japan, and France. And, finally, among *The Coloured Baptists of the South* there has recently been formed a mission board which directs its aims to West Africa.

The Methodist Episcopal Church adopted the Missionary Society platform in 1819. The first agents were sent among the North American Indians, but gradually its energies have extended to Mexico, South America, West Africa, China, Corea, and India.

As some of the American Societies give much attention to the Mohammedan lands lying south and east of the Mediterranean, so this one does in small missions in Norway, Sweden, Denmark, Germany, Switzerland, Italy, Bulgaria, and among the emigrants from Europe, in North and South America. Its strength, however, is given to foreign missions since of its total number of 225 American male and female missionaries, only 19 are in Europe. India is its principal sphere, and has a third of its agency. Its foreign income has steadily risen from £164 in 1820 to £31,646 in 1886.

There are also the following kindred Societies, most of which are small and conduct home as well as foreign missions.

The Methodist Episcopal Church, South, with an advancing income of £44,420, sustains 84 missionaries in China, Mexico, Brazil, and among the Indians.

The African Methodist Episcopal Church, with an income only of £855, has small missions in British Guiana, Hayti, St. Domingo, and Africa.

The African Methodist Episcopal Zion Church has a small mission in Liberia.

The Evangelical Association has an income of £3550, and agents in Japan, Germany, and Switzerland.

The United Brethren in Christ have a mission in Africa.

The Methodist Protestant Church, one in Japan.

And four Methodist bodies in Canada, recently and wisely united, sustain agents in Japan, Bermuda, and among the Indians.

Reference will be found elsewhere to the varied, peculiar, and independent missions founded by Bishop Taylor of the Methodist Episcopal Church, in South America, India, and Central Africa. His zeal, energy, and self-denial, are undoubted, but much diversity of opinion exists respecting the wisdom and propriety of his methods. His somewhat loose relations to the Methodist Episcopal body, calls for this brief notice of his work in this place.

The Board of Missions of the Protestant Episcopal Church, was formed in 1820, and re-organised in 1835. For some years it was a home mission society only, but, in

1830, it entered on a series of attempts, more interesting than successful, to infuse life and truth into the lapsed Christian communities of Greece and Turkey. More recently its efforts have been directed to Africa, China, Japan, and the West Indies. Its resources are far below what those of such an influential Church should be, the income for 1886 being £53,135. But the women of the Church contribute more generously to special objects. Thus, to domestic and foreign missions, freedmen, and Indians, they gave £7521, whilst to other objects a sum equal to £40,572.

The Reformed Episcopal Church has no foreign mission of its own, but gives considerable aid to the "Women's Union Missionary Society for Heathen Lands."

The Presbyterian Societies are numerous, and some of them are distinguished for great zeal and liberality. It is difficult, in several instances, to define wherein they differ, or to discriminate the spheres of some from others. Happily there is a desire on the part of some to combine in foreign work, and if this were carried yet farther, and developed into organic unions, both at home and abroad, the world would be instructed, the Church strengthened, and missions conducted with greater efficiency, economy, and success.

The Presbyterians united with the Congregationalists in mission work until 1837, when *The Board of Foreign Missions of the Presbyterian Church* was formed. *North* has since been added to its designation, to distinguish it from kindred Societies. Its first missionaries were sent to North-Western India, which, with 35 missionaries, yet remains its most important sphere. Next comes China, with 36; then Japan, with 12; the Indian territory, 15; Syria, 13; Africa, 8; Persia, 10; Mexico, 8; Siam, 11; Corea, 1; and Guatemala, 1. It has also 298 American ladies, and 30 laymen in its wide and varied spheres, and more than 1000 native assistants, 122 of them being ordained.

Some of its missions are of great importance, and under

the direction of very competent men. The results are usually varied and solid rather than great.

The order in which the various Societies subsequently arose, with their relative strength, may be seen in the Table given on pages 58 and 59; here it seems best to group and indicate them on another principle.

The United Presbyterian Church of North America has also its most important missions in North-Western India and in Egypt.

The Reformed Presbyterians in the United States have small missions in Syria and Tarsus, and purpose forming others in China and Africa.

The Reformed Church, formerly called Dutch, wisely concentrates its energies in South India, China, and Japan, in all which it has important spheres efficiently managed.

The Reformed Presbyterian General Synod was for more than forty years associated with the first-named Presbyterian Church in its Indian work; now it has a small distinct mission at Rurki, in the same Province.

The Foreign Missionary Presbyterian Board, South, was a secession from the first-named Board, in 1861, on the question of slavery. With an income of £14,634, it sustains twenty-five missionaries in China, Japan, Greece, Italy, Brazil, Mexico, and among the Indians.

The Cumberland Presbyterians are Arminian in doctrine. They are found principally in the Mississippi valley, and have two missionaries in Japan, and six among the Indians.

The *German* settlers in the United States have Societies of their own.

The *Reformed (German) Church*, with an income of £1300, has small missions in Japan, and Bisrampur, India.

The Evangelical Lutherans—General Synod, labour in India.

The Evangelical Lutherans—General Council, among the

Telugu population of Eastern India. They also have a small, promising mission, in the district around Rajahmundry, India.

The Friends, since 1865, have had an active organisation, which, separately, or in connection with the English Friends, combine in foreign work. They have, in Jamaica, 5 missionaries; Mexico, 10; Constantinople, 1; Syria and Palestine, 8; China, 2; at Hoshangabad and in India, 9; in Madagascar, 19; South Africa, 2; and in Japan, 2. Women, and several doctors, are here included. The schools, printing, and benevolent agencies generally, are of a superior order. Their paid native agents number 196. The scholars in their schools, 18,050. The income of their foreign mission agency for 1886, was £21,400. This is an advance throughout.

The Canadian Presbyterians, with an income of £13,890, maintain separately, or in harmony with other co-religionists, eighteen missionaries in the New Hebrides, Formosa, India, Trinidad, and among the Indians.

Five features of the American Societies, generally, require notice—

1. The unhappy multiplication of Societies among the Presbyterians and Methodists, is perplexing to the inquirer, must be attended with rivalry and friction, and an unnecessary amount of expense.

2. The Societies generally combine missions to pagan races and men of European descent, as do the English Methodists' Societies.

3. The Mohammedan world and Eastern Christian communities receive much more attention from American than from European Societies, but the results, especially in the former direction, are not encouraging.

The *Turkish Mission Aid Society* gives them all the assistance in its power from British sources.

4. Women's Missions have greatly increased in number

TABLE OF AMERICAN MISSIONARY SOCIETIES.

When Founded.	Name of Society.	American Missionaries.	Lay Missionaries.	Female Missionaries.	Ordained Native Missionaries.	Native Preachers.	Communicants.	Income.
								£
1810	American Board of Commissioners for Foreign Missions (Congregational),	159	14	261	151	1813	26,129	131,565
1814	American Baptist Missionary Union,	96	6	130	351	1331	118,331	76,999
1819	Missionary Society of the Methodist Episcopal Church, North America,	118	31	143	328	1649	39,873	81,446
1835	Board of Missions of the Protestant Episcopal Church in the United States of North America,	16	7	28	39	158	1,436	53,133
1836	Free Will Baptist Foreign Mission Society,	5	...	14	10	10	558	3,690
1837	Board of Foreign Missions Presbyterian Church, North America,	172	29	297	122	895	20,294	149,032
1847	Seventh Day Baptist Missionary Society,	3	...	3	3	10	145	812
1845	Foreign Mission Board Southern Baptist Convention,	31	...	30	19	44	5,586	16,770
1846	Foreign Mission Board Methodist Episcopal Church, South America,	73	...	11	87	52	9,408	44,425
1845	American Missionary Association,	6	3	30	2	87	348	14,497
1853	Foreign Mission Board United Brethren in Christ,	7	...	7	20	27	3,267	6,959
1853	Foreign Mission Board Reformed Dutch Church, America,	21	1	28	8	188	2,394	16,277
1859	Foreign Mission Board United Presbyterian Church, North America,	16	...	29	11	295	4,019	17,270
1859	Foreign Mission Reformed Presbyterian Church of North America,	3	...	4	...	43	150	3,277
1862	Foreign Mission Presbyterian Church, South,	25	...	29	14	34	1,616	14,634

TABLE OF AMERICAN MISSIONARY SOCIETIES—continued.

When Founded.	Name of Society.	American Missionaries.	Lay Missionaries.	Female Missionaries.	Ordained and Native Missionaries.	Native Preachers.	Communicants.	Income.
1839	Evangelical Lutheran Synod,	5	...	6	3	24	4,789	6,354
1869	Evangelical Lutheran Mission General Synod Council,	5	...	4	3	63	734	3,268
1849	Foreign Christian Missionary Society (Disciples of Christ), Baptist,	20	...	16	6	9	1,905	12,911
1876	Foreign Mission Cumberland Presbyterian Church,*	8	...	5	10	25	1,141	1,894
1878	Foreign Mission Evangelical Association,	5	...	6	4	5	9,114	3,658
1880	Foreign Mission Methodist Protestant Church,	2	...	4	0	3	55	1,700
1878	Foreign Mission African Methodist Episcopal Church,	26	...	5	1	9	734	852
	African Methodist Zion Church,						220	
1875	Associate Reformed Synod, South,	1	...	1	...	6	129	407
1880	Mennonites Mission in North America,	2	...	2	...	13	...	2,500
1836	Reformed Presbyterian General Synod,	1	...	1	...	7	9	377
1795	American Friends' Mission,	29	...	45	...	196	4,746	21,400
1879	Mission of the Reformed Episcopal Church, United States,	Assists the Women's Union Missionary Society, &c.						
1881	Tunker's Missionary Society,	1	...	1	...	3	51	...
1840	Welsh Presbyterians, U.S.,	9	1	...	16	...	893	5,200
1824	Methodist Church of Canada,	56	...	...	9	80	5,046	13,842
1844	Presbyterian Church in Canada,	18	2	25	5	147	2,126	12,154
1866	Canadian Baptist Missionary Society,	8	...	11	13	42	1,987	6,122
	Church of England in Canada,	...	...	...	...	...	...	1,147

* Arminian, found almost exclusively in the Mississippi Valley.

and influence, and the general Societies have a far greater proportion of female agents than those of Europe.

5. Auxiliary agencies, in the form of Bible, Tract, and Medical Societies, are scarcely less efficient than they are here, whilst the literature which informs and feeds the missionary spirit, is far superior to our own.

CONTINENTAL EUROPE.

The zeal which distinguished some of the Danes, Germans, and Dutch, during the sixteenth, seventeenth, and early part of the eighteenth century, greatly declined about the middle of the latter century. It would be suggestive to trace at length the causes of the change, but briefly they may be thus indicated.

The movement originally was, in no instance but that of the Moravians, a popular or general one. It arose with eminently consecrated men, such as Hans Egede, and C. T. Francke of Halle; or illustrious men, such as Frederic IV. of Denmark, and Count Zinzendorf; or with Governments, formal, selfish, and exclusive, as that of Holland. And when the individual men died, on whom almost all depended, there was seldom an Elisha to receive the mantle of Elijah. Persons there were of zeal and piety, ready to respond to the call of a great leader; but the leader was wanting; and whilst the churches were too formal, cold, and unspiritual to adopt a mission policy, individuals were too much fettered by the existing ecclesiastical or political conditions to form Societies such as now exist, or themselves to enter on the work.

Thus it came to pass that when the pietist fervour of the end of the seventeenth and beginning of the eighteenth century subsided, the missionary spirit springing from it declined, and the noble work originated by men like Lütkens and Francke in Europe, and Ziegenbalg and Baldæus abroad, was practically left to die out, or to be feebly sustained by English aid, before the close of last century.

One Church only, and that the smallest and poorest, sustained its mission zeal, in spite of the Rationalism which so generally blighted the goodly promise of a mission era on the continent, just one hundred years before its dawn in England. "In twenty years—from 1735 to 1756—the Moravian Church called into being more missions than the whole evangelical Church in two centuries. During the century, its magnificent energy sustained the missions already planted, and formed new ones; so that this Church of less than 35,000 souls, had in 1800, in twelve countries, twenty-six stations, with eighty missionaries. Now it has missions in Greenland, Labrador, Alaska, North America, the West India islands of St. Thomas, St. Croix, St. Kitts, Jamaica, Antigua, Barbadoes, Tobago; on the Moskito Coast, Demerara, Surinam, South, West, and East Africa, Thibet, and Australia. Its stations are 118; missionaries, 335 (174 men, 161 women); native helpers, 1611; communicants, 29,283; baptised adherents, 83,052." Some features of the missions deserve notice. Usually they are small, and placed among sparse, decaying, and uninfluential races. Since they were formed, more than one hundred and forty years ago, in twelve of the countries where now they are found, the results in self-support, communicants, and adherents, are disappointing. This is, in part, owing to the isolation and poverty of the people, and in some measure to the inelastic constitution of the Brotherhood, which is not attractive to most races. It is not so easy of explanation, that with its fraternal principles, faith in the work of the Holy Spirit, irrespective of human training for service, and its lengthened experience, its native helpers should not number more, and its native ministers only 41. But the self-denial, the heroism, the faith, the patience, and the humility alike of the Church and the missionaries, and the manner in which they have tenaciously persevered in some spheres, in spite of discouragements and difficulties, is worthy of the utmost admiration and respect. The mission resources of the Brethren are largely derived from British and American sources,* and they are expended with exemplary care; for the home expenditure on the income is only 3½ per cent.

The Dutch,

At the close of last century, were the first on the Continent to follow the lead of England in the formation of a missionary society. This was the *Netherlands Society*, founded at Rotterdam in 1797. It was at first little more than a foreign auxiliary to the London Missionary Society, whose great catholic principles it adopted. Its first recruits, Vanderkemp and Kitcherer, became admirable agents of the English Society, but in 1813 it sent its own first missionary, J. Kam, to Amboyna, and subsequently adopted Java, Timor, Soombaya, and the Celebes as its spheres. Resembling the London Society, it has an unusually large number of communicants, and, like that Society, the far greater number—85,000 out of 98,943—are found in the province of one island, the one last named.

After a long interval, several other Societies were formed. They are all small, have their spheres in Dutch possessions, and since their management is coloured by the reticence which distinguishes all Dutch colonial affairs, our information respecting them is limited.

The Java Committee, formed in 1859, has an income of about £1229, with 15 European agents in Java and Sumatra.

The Ermelo Missionary Society was formed in 1846,

---

* The Continent of Europe, £7373, 9s. 6d.; Great Britain and Ireland, £3925, 2s. 4d.; North America, £2301, 7s. 6d; West Indies and Surinam, £143, 16s. 4d.; Legacies and Interest, £5325, 11s. 4d.; Total, £19,069, 7s. 6d.

on a basis similar to that adopted by Müller of Bristol, in the prosecution of his charitable and religious work. Its foreign efforts are confined to Central Java and Calioub, near Cairo.

The Netherlands Union, 1858, with £2630 income, sustains 14 foreign agents among the Soondanees of West Java.

The Utrecht Society, 1859, has £3988 income, and 15 missionaries in Bali, Almahira, and New Guinea.

The Dutch Reformed Society, 1860, income £1160, has stations in Java.

The Christian Reformed Churches Society seceded from the former, and conducts a mission of its own in Java.

The Mennonites, since 1880, have had 8 missionaries in Java, chiefly engaged in literary and industrial pursuits.

To these must be added an important *Auxiliary to the Rhenish Missionary Society*, formed in 1860, and contributing annually about £1000 to its funds; and an *Auxiliary to the Moravian Society*, formed at Zeist near Utrecht in 1792, and therefore the oldest missionary organisation in Holland. It has a special field of its own in Surinam, where at 14 stations there are 36 missionaries, 162 native assistants, 2100 scholars, and 25,043 church members. Apparently it is exceptionally vigorous and successful.

Mr. Grattan Guinness, after careful personal inquiry in Holland, thus summarises the state of the missions: "I gathered that the various Dutch Societies support 146 missionaries, of whom 70 are in the West and 76 in the East Indies. Connected with these missions are 208 teachers and 498 native assistants. There are 190 schools with 10,866 scholars, and 76 stations. The total receipts for all missions is between £26,000 and £27,400."

GERMANY

Has thirteen Societies, some of which are of considerable importance.

The Moravian Society, the first in age, importance, and interest, has been already described.

The Basel Society, though located in Switzerland, derives most of its funds and agents from Germany. In constitution it somewhat resembles the London Missionary Society, and unites the Lutheran and Reformed Evangelicals of Switzerland and Germany.

It arose out of an earnest attempt, about 1780, to promote true piety and evangelical doctrine, which caught the missionary fire from the Societies formed a few years later in England. At first subscriptions only were urged for the missions conducted from Halle, Herrnhut, and London; but in 1815 a mission school was formed to train missionaries for existing Societies, since Germans in considerable numbers volunteered for such service. This Institution developed, in 1822, into the Basel Society. Its first independent enterprises in Persia and the Russian Caucasus were not wisely chosen, and were abandoned in 1834; but its subsequent aims, first in West Africa, then in 1834 in India, and very recently in China, have met with much success. It has now in those spheres 175 missionaries, 8380 communicants, more than 17,000 adherents, and an income of about £37,900.

The Berlin Society, or the Society for the Promotion of Evangelical Missions among the Heathen, was formed in 1824, as the result of an appeal from Neander, Tholuck, and others. Its first enterprise, after some delay, was the formation of a training seminary similar to that at Basel, which, after educating some eighty agents for various societies, was dissolved about 1829. Its own missionaries were first sent out in 1834 to South Africa, where, after reverse and discouragement among the Bechuanas, a good amount of success has crowned their endeavours. Among the Koranas and Zulus, it is still the "day of small things." Recently it has sent several agents to China. In the spheres indicated it has 53 male and 30 female missionaries, 8260 communicants, and 14,000 adherents, with an income of £18,500. It is an essentially Lutheran Society.

In 1836, Pastor, or, as he is often called, *Father Gossner*, withdrew from the Berlin Society, and formed another, usually known by his name. His leading ideas—and he threw his personality entirely into the Society—were, that missionaries should, as soon as possible, support themselves by trade, and that, as artisan missionaries were to be encouraged, a scientific theological training was not essential. With great energy, some tact, and much force of will, he ruled the Missionary Union, as it was called. In ten years he sent out eighty missionaries to Australia, India, Dutch India, West Africa, and North America. Most of these, however, ceased to be missionaries, or joined other Societies, and some of the missions were abandoned. After his death, in 1852, his Society, for such it really was, greatly modified its policy, and now confines its energies almost entirely to the Indian Provinces of Behar and Chota Nagpore. Among the aboriginal Kolls, its success at first was great, though the early promise of former years has not been perpetuated. Its 32 missionaries have in charge a Christian community of 30,000 souls, of whom 12,850 are communicants. Its last reported income was £6700.

The Rhenish Society has an interesting history. Beginning simply as a Prayer Union for Missions to the Heathen, it went on to publish accounts of Mission work, then developed into a Bible, then a Tract, then a Missionary Society to the Jews, then into a Missionary Training Seminary, and finally into a Foreign Missionary Society. Its centre is at Barmen, and its constitution is sufficiently free to unite Lutherans and the Reformed in harmonious co-operation. Its first missionaries were sent, in 1829, to South Africa. Then, in 1834, it extended its agencies to Borneo. In 1862, to Sumatra. In 1865, to Nias, a neighbouring island, and, in 1846, to China. The latter is its smallest mission, and South Africa, including Cape Colony, Namaqualand, and Damaraland, its largest. Altogether, it has, at 52 stations, 76 male missionaries, 280 native helpers, 25,000 converts, of whom 9375 are communicants, and 5000 scholars. Its last reported income was £16,560.

The Evangelical Lutheran Society, often called from its locale the *Leipsic Missionary Society*, is a strict Lutheran organisation. Moving off gradually from the Basel Society, it assumed an independent existence in 1836. After some time it concentrated its aims on Southern India, attempting to enter on various fields occupied by the Danish Halle Missions of the eighteenth century, which had not been adopted by the Church and Propagation Societies. Its principal stations are at Tranquebar, Trichinopoly, Madras, and Arcot. With 24 male missionaries, and 11 native ministers, it has a baptised community of 15,000, and of these, as many as 13,321 are communicants. In the English Societies, the proportion of the latter to the former is about 1 to 4.

The North German Society also had its origin in 1836. It has had some difficulties to contend with on account of creed and confessional questions. Now its home is at Bremen. In general policy it follows the Basel Society. Its first missionaries were sent to New Zealand, in 1842, and, since 1847, it has had agents with the Ewe tribe, on the Gold Coast, West Africa. Its missionaries are 11, its converts 700, and its income £4000 to £4800 a year.

The Hermannsberg Mission, like Gossner's, owes its existence to one man. Harms, pastor of the Hermannsberg Church, becoming dissatisfied with the policy of the North German Societies, founded the one in question, on a close Lutheran basis, and for the purpose of sending out mission colonies; though the latter, as a principle, has been abandoned. Its first detachment, of 20 labourers, settled among the

Gallas of East Africa, in 1853, and since, whilst sustaining this mission, it has extended its energies to Australia, New Zealand, Arcot, and Telingana, in South-Eastern India. Altogether, it has 42 ordained, and 48 lay missionaries, with 4420 communicants, and 10,640 baptised adherents. Its annual income is about £10,000.

Other German Missionary Societies may be more briefly described:—

The St. Chrischona Missionary Society, or *Pilgrim's Mission*, was formed, near Basel, in 1848. Its spheres are, an orphanage in Jerusalem, and small missions at Feodosia, South Russia, and among the Gallas of East Africa.

The Brecklum, or Schleswig, Society was founded in 1878. It has no separate Missions of its own, but aids an independent Mission in India.

The Women's Union for the Christian Education of Women in the East, has sent about twenty ladies to India, Palestine, and South Africa, since its formation in 1842, though its income is less than £100 annually.

The Knacks Women's Missionary Union for China has, since 1850, sustained an orphan and foundling house at Hong-Kong.

The Kaiserswerth's Deaconesses Institute is directly and indirectly doing much good by the agency of about eighty ladies in hospitals, orphanages, and schools. Originated by Pastor Fliedner, near Dusseldorf, from small beginnings, in 1836, it has come to exert a wide influence in an important sphere. It has sent out 6000 nurses, and caused the formation of sixty-nine similar institutions. It has an admirable institution at Beirut, Syria, and many of its deaconesses are in Egypt.

This year an important new Society has been formed in Berlin, as the result of growing interest in missions, and of German colonising zeal. It is called the *East African Society*. The operations of this Society are to be confined to German territory in South Equatorial Africa and Somali Land. It will alike care for the German settlers, for Mohammedans, and the heathen. A Women's Association has been formed in connection with it, to send German ladies to assist in the work, which will be medical, educational, and evangelistic. Already the first missionaries have been sent out.

France

Has one Protestant Missionary Society.

The Paris Evangelical Missionary Society was formed in 1822. With an income of about £11,500, it sustains about thirty-one ordained and lay agents in Basutoland, on the Senegal, and in Tahiti. The first is its most important sphere, where it has gathered at least 12,000 converts. By an amicable arrangement some years ago, it took the place of the London Missionary Society in Tahiti. Recently one of its most enterprising missionaries has left Basutoland to found a new mission eastward on the Zambesi. And now, wisely, it is seeking to begin work in the extensive French possessions on the Congo.

Switzerland

Has two Missionary Societies.

The Evangelical Society of Geneva, like our Turkish Missions Aid Society, has no missions entirely its own, but acts as a feeder and auxiliary to other Societies.

The Missions of the Free Church of the Canton de Vaud, formed in 1869, has five ordained and three lay missionaries, who are successfully labouring among the Magwambas of South Africa.

Northern Europe

Has seven small interesting Missionary Societies.

The Danish Lutheran Society was formed in 1821. After acting as an auxiliary to the Basel Society, it began, in 1861, a small mission in the Arcot district of Southern India, attracted there by the hallowed associations of the previous century. More recently it has rendered valuable aid to the Greenland Mission, though the number of its agents, including ministers, laymen, and women, is but fourteen.

The Swedish Society was formed in 1835, and was for some years chiefly a contributing agency to other Societies; but in 1855 it was incorporated with *The Lunds Missionary Society*, which had been formed in 1845. Since 1876 the united Societies have become identified with the Swedish National Church.

Recently there has been formed *The Swedish National League*. But little definite information can be given of these Societies, excepting that about fifteen Swedish missionaries labour in Abyssinia, Zululand, and the Central Provinces of India.

The Norwegian Society was formed at Stavangar in 1842. Its first stations were in Natal and Zululand; but, since 1867, it has entered Madagascar, with a large force and considerable success. The extent of these is described elsewhere.

The Finnish Missionary Society was formed in 1859, and has an annual income of about £4000. It wisely co-operates with the Rhenish Society, though having a separate mission in Ovampoland, in South-West Africa. Its results are not encouraging.

The British, American, and European Societies which we have mentioned, though the principal, are not the only ones.*
What we have done is indicative rather than exhaustive. The rise, main features, and present strength of the leading

* See "Outline of the History of Protestant Missions," p. 65. By Dr. Warneck.

Societies only have been indicated, but the following remarks will assist to give completeness to our review:—

1. It is a gratifying sign that Missions grow out of colonisation.

The United States afford the finest illustration of this, but the British Colonies follow the same noble example. In many instances they attend not only to the spiritual wants of their own people and the aborigines around them, but co-operate with English Societies, or form similar ones of their own, to reach races entirely pagan.

CANADA

has four such Missionary Societies.

The Presbyterian Missionary Society, East, has a small mission in Trinidad, and along with Scotch, Australian, and New Zealand Presbyterians, it helps to sustain the interesting though trying work of God which is being carried on in the New Hebrides.

The Presbyterian Missionary Society, West, has small Missions in India, China, and among the North American Indians.

The Methodist Missionary Society has agents in Japan and among the Indians.

The Baptist Missionary Society has agents in South-Eastern India.

AUSTRALIA.

The Australian churches contribute commendably to the Missionary Societies of the mother country, and some of them desire to undertake distinct work of their own. The Wesleyan Methodists have already assumed the responsibility of sustaining Missions in some of the Australian and Polynesian islands.

SOUTH AFRICA.

The Dutch Settlers in South Africa have recently formed a missionary organisation.

2. Individual and isolated effort, which so largely characterised Christian Missions all through the seventeenth and eighteenth centuries, and then almost entirely disappeared, is now seen revived again in various forms, and in largely increased vigour.

(a) The Friends, for instance, who all along their history have evinced a desire to enter on individual Missions, have found it advisable to combine, since 1867, in a Foreign Mission Society.

So, also, the Congo Mission, which was founded by Mr. and Mrs. Grattan Guinness, has altogether outgrown private resources, and has been entrusted to the American Baptist Missionary Union.

It is not necessary to define the precise position of the China Inland Mission. Begun in faith and prayer by Mr. Hudson Taylor, and conducted with rare unselfishness and devotion, chiefly by him and Mr. Broomhall, it, too, as already mentioned on a preceding page, is in process of active development.

(b) Some Missions commenced by personal zeal retain an independent or semi-independent position of necessity, or from motives of expediency. Thus it is with Miss Whateley's schools in Egypt, and some of the agencies in Syria.

(c) But the greater number of independent Missions are of more recent origin, and are isolated because the society idea is rejected on principle.

We give a catalogue of such Missions, but it is of necessity incomplete, since their friends profess to avoid publicity, in some instances publish no report, and decline to furnish statistical information.

The Tables of the various Missionary Societies which we now proceed to give* will be better understood in the light of the remarks which follow these Tables.

* For other Tables see pp 178-186.

TABLE OF CONTINENTAL MISSIONARY SOCIETIES.

When Founded	Name of Society.	Ordained European Missionaries.	Lay Missionaries.	Female Missionaries.	Ordained Native Missionaries.	Other Native Preachers.	Adherents.	Communicants.	Income.
	Dutch.								£
1797	Netherlands Missionary Society,	12	6	9	4	209	...	98,943	7,950
1841	Ermelo Missionary Society,	3	2	23	...	5	...	60	910
1859	Java Comité,	5	4	6	...	16	...	61	1,227
1858	Missionary Union of the Netherlands,	7	...	7	...	28	...	793	2,630
1859	Dutch Reformed Church Missionary Society,	3	...	2	...	12	...	300	1,150
1860	Christian Reformed Missionary Society,	4	...	2	...	5	...	60	136
1859	Utrecht Missionary Society,	5	4	6	...	16	...	61	3,988
1869	Mennonite Missionary Society,	3	2	3	...	12	...	100	2,020
	The following are Auxiliaries to the two Societies named, and their statistics are included in the parent Society, but they are named here to add completeness to our Tables:—								
1792	Zeist (near Utrecht) Auxiliary to the Moravian Missionary Society,	36	...	...	...	162	...	25,043	604
1860	Auxiliary to the Rhenish Missionary Society,	31	...	...	...	24	...	332	960
	German.								
1732	Moravian Missionary Society,	174	...	161	27	1,584	83,462	29,283	19,069
1815	Basel Evangelical Missionary Society,	76	26	73	30	298	17,053	8,380	37,973
1823	Rhenish Missionary Society,	70	6	60	2	280	25,000	9,375	16,559
1836	North German Missionary Society,	11	...	9	...	20	700	275	4,150
1836	Gossner's Missionary Union,	14	5	12	11	210	30,000	12,850	6,700
1836	Berlin Missionary Society,	45	8	30	2	337	14,000	8,260	18,424

TABLE OF CONTINENTAL MISSIONARY SOCIETIES—*Continued*.

When Founded.	Name of Society.	Ordained European Missionaries.	Lay Missionaries.	Female Missionaries.	Ordained Native Missionaries.	Other Native Preachers.	Adherents.	Communicants.	Income.
	GERMAN—*continued.*								£
1836	Leipsic Lutheran Missionary Society,	22	2	22	11	238	15,000	13,589	17,440
1842	Pilgrim Society at St. Chrischona,	5	26	6	...	12	...	...	5,131
1849	Missionary Society of Herrnannsberg,	42	48	40	22	50	10,640	4,420	10,000
1877	Missionary Society of Schleswig-Holstein,	...	...	...	...	...	...	...	...
	FRENCH.								
1822	Paris Evangelical Missionary Society,	25	6	26	2	130	...	6,820	11,200
	SWISS.								
1869	Free Church, Canton de Vaud,	5	3	7	6	9	...	100	2,319
	NORWEGIAN.								
1842	Norwegian Missionary Society,	37	3	16	10	350	38,000	3,760	10,570
	SWEDISH.								
1853	Stockholm Stads Mission,	4	...	3	...	2	...	300	900
1845	Lunds Missionary Society,	7	2	4	...	14	...	80	1,450
1865	Ansgarius Union,	1	...	1	...	...	...	20	424
	DANISH.								
1821	Danish Evangelical Lutheran Missionary Society,	7	2	5	1	20	...	109	1,600
	FINNISH.								
1859	Finnish Missionary Society,	5	3	7	...	6	...	18	4,030

TABLE OF INDEPENDENT FOREIGN MISSIONS, 1884-85.

Missions.	Missionaries Ordained.	Lay.	Women.	Native Workers Ordained.	Others.	Native Communicants.	Native Pupils.	Mission Income.
1. Misses Anstey and Read's Mission, Southern India,	..	..	2	..	..	2	350	£1,200
2. Ghazipur Mission, North-West Provinces,	2	..	1	..	3	250	80	1,160
3. Mrs. Munford's Mission, Bulgaria,	..	..	2	..	2	..	..	494
4. Basim Faith Mission, Western India,	1	..	10	..	..	2	20	400
5. Joppa (Jaffa) Mission,	..	..	2	..	..	2	60	...
6. Joppa, Miss Arnott's Mission,	1	..	4	..	5	..	44	1,500
7. C. B. Ward's Mission, South-East India,	1	4	4	..	5	50	100	1,750
8. Ellichpoor Mission, Central Provinces, India,	1	..	1	..	..	..	..	100
9. Abbotsford Mission, Ceylon,	..	..	..	..	1	30	35	...
10. Bethal Santhal Mission,	1	..	2	..	25	180	320	300
11. Indian Home Mission, Santhalisthan,	2	4	4	4	66	4,083	2,960	3,800
12. Ooloobeniya, Southern Bengal, India,	..	..	..	..	..	..	..	174
13. Brazil Christian Union,	1	..	1	..	1	39	..	...
14. Miss Whately's Mission, Egypt,	..	..	1	..	6	..	600	100
15. Korkoo Mission, Central India,	1	..	1	..	1	8	20	10,000
16. Bishop Taylor's Mission (India),	50	55	30	..	10	3,220	3,250	8,000
Do. do. (South America),	12	25	20	..	12	..	200	8,000
Do. do. (Africa),	10	25	20	..	..	..	50	...
17. Gopalgunge Mission, Bengal,	..	..	..	1	5	45	256	160
18. Akola Mission, Central India,	4	2	5	..	1	20	20	405
19. Mary A. Sharp's Kroo Mission, Liberia,	..	..	1	..	2	25	25	100
20. Anna E. Morris's Mission, Liberia,	..	..	1	..	2	..	40	100
21. Robert L. Harris's Mission, Liberia,	1	..	2	..	..	..	..	100
22. Robert Shemeld's Mission, Natal,	1	..	1	..	..	..	..	120
23. Inhambane Mission, South Africa,	1	..	1	..	..	..	..	200

1. The preceding Tables, and those given at the end of the book include only such Societies as labour among Pagan and Mohammedan races; therefore Missionary Societies to Jews Roman Catholics, and the British Colonies are excluded, however excellent and necessary their work may be.

2. In considering the funds and agencies of Societies whose spheres of labour are Colonial and Continental as well as Foreign, such as, for instance, the Gospel Propagation and most of the Methodist Missionary Societies, we have given, as nearly as possible, the figures relating to their work in heathen lands only, so far as we have been able to separate one from the other.

3. The names of some of the smaller Societies which we have given, are auxiliary to or in close association with other Societies, such as the Gospel Propagation and Church Missionary Societies; they have usually therefore no separate statistics except with regard to income.

4. The principles on which various Societies base their statistics vary greatly. This applies to the exclusiveness or inclusiveness of native ministers, preachers, church members, adherents, and stations. Thus, though the figures given are substantially correct, a different interpretation would be given, in some instances, to figures under the same designation.

5. This applies especially to the least definite of the numbers given in their statistics—that of lady missionaries. Some include under this term the wives of all the missionaries, as well as the ladies who have been definitely sent out to engage in medical, zenana, and school work—a method both erroneous and misleading.

6. Though the number of the Societies is large, it is important, in forming an accurate judgment of the Foreign Missionary enterprise, to bear in mind that many of them occupy very restricted spheres, and have but limited resources. A large number, for instance, have a smaller income than £4000 a year, and fewer than 20 missionaries.

7. To form an accurate judgment respecting the amount annually raised for Foreign Missions, attention should be given not simply to the sum total, but also to the sources from whence it is derived. Even churches and denominations may credit themselves with too much zeal and liberality. For instance, Dr. Grundemann, to whose carefully prepared tables we are much indebted, greatly reduces the sum apparently raised for this work by 24 British Missionary Societies in 1886, by deducting the following sums which are not British contributions:—

Received from the Colonies	£21,495
,, Invested funds	118,912
,, Mission stations	41,201
,, Educational grants	5,821
,, Germany	3,923

These sums, deducted from the aggregate income of our Societies, presents our zeal and liberality on behalf of Missions in a diminished aspect. And the inference is a correct one. Thus in this instance—as in so many others—our liberality is less than we assume it to be.

8. The total sum thus contributed may properly be viewed in various lights. For what a stupendous and important purpose is this money contributed! How many givers and what kind of gifts does it represent? How does it compare with other forms of expenditure—voluntary, necessary, and compulsory? How much do the givers retain after parting with their gifts to this cause? Some aspects of these questions will be considered in another chapter, here only one of them may be noticed.

Granting the largest estimate of £2,400,000 to be the sum contributed. It is drawn from a Protestant population of not less than 130 millions for the conversion of 1030 millions who are not Christians, and who have none of the principles, hopes, and impulses which Christianity inspires. This means no more than 4⅖d. per head—a small sum indeed from those who have all derived from Christianity the blessings of civilisation at the least, and a large proportion of whom believe it to be the only true and divine revelation of God to man.

The following analysis of what is given in America is suggestive and humiliating. Is our British giving to Missions greater?

"According to Dr Dorchester, there were, in 1880, ten million members of Evangelical Protestant Churches in the United States who, from 1870 to 1880, gave annually for missions, home and foreign, five million five hundred thousand dollars (*i.e.*, £1,100,000), an average of fifty-five cents for each church-member. A considerable proportion, however, is given by church-goers who are not church-members. We will call it, therefore, an even fifty cents (*i.e.*, two shillings) for each of the ten million professing Christians. But many thousands give a dollar each, which means that as many thousands more give nothing. There are some thousands who give ten dollars, and for every thousand of this class there are nineteen thousand who do not give anything. Some give five thousand dollars, and for each of them there are ten thousand church-members who do not give one cent to redeem the heathen world, for which He with whom they profess to be in sympathy gave His life.

"Five million five hundred thousand dollars for missions sounds like a large sum. But great and small are relative terms. Compared with the need of the work and the ability of the Church, it is pitiable indeed. Look at that ability. The Christian religion, by rendering men temperate, industrious, and moral, makes them prosperous. There are but few of the very poor in our churches. The great question has come to be—'How can we reach the masses?' Church-membership is made up chiefly of the well-to-do and the rich. On the other hand, a majority of the membership is composed of women, who control less money than men. It is, therefore, fair to say that the church-member is at least as well off as the average citizen. One-fifth, then, of the wealth of the United States, or eight billion seven hundred and twenty-eight million four hundred thousand dollars (*i.e.*, £1,745,680,000) was in the hands of church-members in 1880, and this takes no account of the immense capital in brains and muscles. Of this great wealth *one-sixteenth part of one per cent.*, or one dollar out of fifteen hundred and eighty-six, is given in a year for the salvation of a thousand million heathen. If Christians spent every cent of wages, salary, and other income on themselves, and gave to missions only one cent on the dollar (*i.e.*, about one half-farthing in the shilling) of their real and personal property, their contribution would be eighty-seven million two hundred and eighty-four thousand dollars (*i.e.*, £17,456,800) instead of five million five hundred thousand dollars (£1,100,000). In 1880 they paid out nearly six times as much for sugar and molasses as for the world's salvation; seven times as much for boots and shoes; sixteen times as much for cotton and woollen goods; eleven times as much for meat; and eighteen times as much for bread. From 1870 to 1880 the average annual increase of the wealth of church-members was three hundred and ninety-one million seven hundred and forty thousand dollars (or £78,348,000). And this, remember, was over and above all expense of living and all benevolences! That is, the average annual increase of wealth in the hands of professed Christians was seventy-one times greater than their offering to missions, home and foreign. How that offering looks when compared with their wealth and its annual increase may be seen by the accompanying diagram." *

Put in another form, the United States spent for liquor in that year £180,000,000; for tobacco, £120,000,000; for missions to the heathen considerably less than three quarters of a million; and for all Christian purposes only £41,000,000. If the people gave but one hundredth part of their real and personal property to Home and Foreign Missions, the amount would rise from what it is now—£1,100,000—to £17,456,600!

* "Our Country." Published by the American Home Mission Society.

DIAGRAM REFERRED TO ON PAGE 78.

[*The amount annually subscribed to Missions by Church members of America is* ONE-SIXTEENTH PART OF ONE PER CENT. *of their annual wealth, and* one seventy-first part of the annual increase *of their wealth.*]

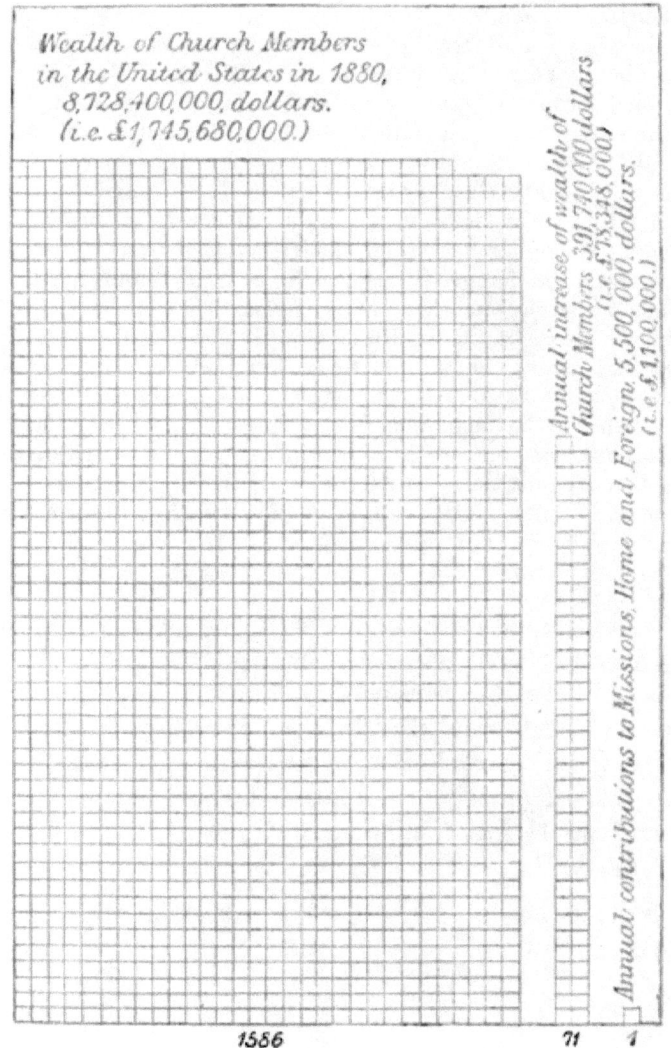

CHAPTER VII.

MISSION FIELDS AND AGENCIES—AFRICA.

THOUGH Africa is nearer to England than America and Asia, we know less of it than either of the other two Continents. It is about 5000 miles in length, and 4600 at its utmost breadth, and has an area of 12,000,000 square miles, whilst that of Great Britain and Ireland is not more than 121,115 square miles. Our information relative to immense regions of the interior of Africa is so vague, that statements respecting the entire population, and their ethnological and religious divisions, are estimates rather than statements of fact.

The entire population is supposed to number 220 millions, speaking about 438 languages, and 163 dialects, and divided in race as follows :—

Negroes,	155,000,000
Hamites,	24,000,000
Bantus,	21,000,000
Foolahs,	10,000,000
Nubians,	2,000,000
Arabs,	5,000,000
Hottentots,	150,000
Jews,	938,000
Europeans,	1,650,000
	219,738,000

Mohammedanism prevails throughout North Africa, and has, in recent years, spread extensively southward. Its adherents are supposed to number 50,416,000.

Christianity exists in its Protestant form in South Africa; as Roman Catholicism in the Portuguese settlements on the West Coast; and in yet more emasculated and corrupt aspects in Egypt and Abyssinia.

Heathenism, in its lowest form, keeps in degradation more than 150 millions of the people.

Many of the political divisions of the "Dark Continent" are so vague, and the respective fields of Missionary labour, especially in its Central portions, extend over such vast tracts of territory, that we shall group our list of African Missions merely under the four general headings of Northern, Central and Western, Southern, and Eastern Africa.

NORTHERN AFRICA,

Including Morocco, Algeria, Tunis, Tripoli, Barca, and Egypt, has a population of about 28 millions. Owing to Mohammedan intolerance, the missions are few and unproductive. In these respects it forms a striking contrast to South Africa, with a much smaller population.

Egypt, once so rich in Christian influence, is now as difficult a sphere for the missionary as the statesman. The former has made less impression here than almost anywhere else. Hocker and Antes, both singularly gifted men, here laboured more than a hundred years ago, and failed almost entirely. More recently, Krapf, Gobat, and other agents of the Church Missionary Society, tried it in vain. At present, the latter Society, the Church of Scotland, the Associate Relief Church, and the Ermelo Society (Dutch), have small missions here. The Chrischona (German) Society has stations and industrial schools in Alexandria, Cairo, and other places along the Nile, and the schools of the Kaiserwerth Deaconesses and of Miss Whately are of great use.

But the most important agency is that of the United Presbyterians of America, begun in 1854, whose centre is in Cairo. They have nine foreign missionaries and seven female teachers, who are aided by a yet greater number of native preachers and teachers. The native adherents are about 2000, in thirteen congregations.

Tripoli and *Barca* are without fixed mission agency. *Tunis* has one small station only.

Algeria has a population of three millions, whose political, race, and religious sentiments are not favourable to Christianity. It is only very recently that missions anywhere have been attempted among them, and hitherto but few signs of success have appeared. A small band of Lutherans, with one coadjutor from Scotland, are aided by native assistants, and conduct fifteen schools, and worship in seventy-one places.

"The mission to the Kabyles and other Berber races of North Africa," has had "male or female agents for three or four years in Kabylia, Constantine, Tlemcen, and Oran." Its skilled medical missionaries are the most appreciated.

Morocco, though almost twice as large as the British Islands, with a population of more than six millions, and the nearest to us of all non-Christian lands, was until four years ago without any definite evangelistic agency. The Rev. E. T. Baldwin, an American Baptist, is now the superintendent of a small independent Mission. Its centre is Tangier, with an out-station at Arzala; but Fez, with its 200,000 inhabitants, has for some time been the scene of Mr. Baldwin's labours, and journeys have been made far into the south, where the Berbers are supposed to be less fanatical than the Moors.

Little has been attempted in all this unpromising field, and the efforts of this new organisation will be watched with interest, not unmixed with apprehension. It has planted a chain of small missions in this unusually trying region, from Tangier to Tunis, a distance of about 1100 miles, "if that indeed can be called a chain, in which there are no stations for several hundred miles. There is no Protestant missionary for about 1000 miles to the east, and 1600 miles to the south—that is, until Abyssinia is reached in the former direction, and the Lower Niger in the latter."

CENTRAL AND WESTERN AFRICA.

South of the States just named is an immense and little known region, including one-third of the entire Continent, and estimated to contain over 100,000,000 people, in which there is but a single Mission. It extends, from the borders of the Nile and Abyssinia, right across the continent to the Atlantic, a distance of 2000 miles, and has a width varying from 600 to 900 miles. Its northern part is barren, thinly populated, and mostly claimed by the States on the Mediterranean, already named. The southern portion — *The Soudan*—extending to Ashantee and the Congo Valley, is covered by a group of kingdoms, some of which are of considerable extent and populousness. General Haig has recently visited Arabia, Abyssinia, and Suakim, to ascertain what openings there were for Christian effort in those countries, and, as might have been anticipated, he reports unfavourably of reaching the Soudanese from the East.

South of the Soudan, on the West Coast, there are at *Rio Pongas*, and on the banks of the *Senegal* and *Gambia*, small missions—the first of a chain extending all down the Coast to Cape Colony, and then northward on the East Coast as far as the Equator.

Sierra Leone, with an area of only 25,000 square miles, and a population of less than 80,000, is more than sufficiently supplied with Christian agencies. The Church Missionary Society and the Wesleyans founded missions in this unhealthy spot,* and among its hybrid population, as

---

* It is mournful evidence of the unhealthiness of the climate, that in the first twenty-two years, the Church Missionary Society sent

early as 1816; and much more recently, the Propagation Society, the Countess of Huntingdon's Connexion, the United Methodists, the American Missionary Association, and the United Brethren, have sent agents there. The first-named Society has 10,000 adherents, of whom 4870 are communicants, and 3600 scholars are in its 44 schools. The Wesleyans in nine circuits have 41 chapels and 22 other preaching places, under the charge of 14 missionaries and assistant missionaries, who are aided by 6 catechists and 113 lay preachers. The church members number 5945, the attendants on public worship 21,900, and the day-scholars 3100.

Liberia has not fulfilled the sanguine hopes of its founders in 1822, or of those who aided to make it an Independent State in 1847. With a coast line of 380 miles, and a territory extending inland from 60 to 100 miles, it has a population of less than 20,000 civilised negroes, with a varied aboriginal population of about 1,050,000. It has more than a necessary supply of Christian agencies, almost entirely American. The Episcopal Methodists took the field in 1833, the Episcopalians in 1834, the Baptists in 1835. Since then the Presbyterians and some independent agencies have formed congregations.

On the *Gold Coast* the Wesleyan and Basel Society are active. The former began here in 1835, and have in this large and populous region all the elements of an efficient mission — 54 chapels, 131 other preaching-places, more than 500 agents and helpers of various kinds, a membership of almost 6000, an attendance at public worship of 18,000, and 2200 scholars.

Farther east, around *Lagos*, they have a similar though smaller series of stations. Their desire is to penetrate into

seventy-nine missionaries to the settlement, where by far the greater number of them shortly died; whilst in the Wesleyan cemetery more than forty missionaries and missionaries' wives rest.

the interior; but Foulah, Ashantee, Dahomey, and the regions beyond, are at present hardly accessible.

In the *Yoruba Country*, to the south-east, the Church Missionary Society has several important stations. At Lagos there are six churches, with large congregations, a training institution, and good schools. Along the coast and in the interior at Abeokuta, Ibadan, and other places, there are considerable bodies of Christians and active evangelistic organisations. It is a good sign that for some years several of the churches have met their own expenses, and been ministered to by pastors of their own race.

On both sides of *the Niger*, and for 400 miles inland, the Church Missionary Society has several large and flourishing stations. Here Bishop Crowther, assisted by two native arch-deacons, has charge of more than 4600 converts, and an important aggressive work is being carried on. "The fields are white already to harvest," says the Bishop. "I can now employ two dozen Christian teachers, lay or clerical, in new localities, from which we receive loud calls for them."

Since 1839, when liberated slaves began to leave Sierra Leone and return to their native homes, and the Church Missionary Society sent among them its first missionary to the Yoruba Country in 1842, and its first to the Niger as recently as 1857, a great change has passed over the whole region. Slavery, human sacrifice, deeds of lawless violence, and heathenism of the most degraded type were general; now they have ceased or are greatly abated. This Society in its West African Missions, including Sierra Leone, has 25,000 professing Christians, and 9000 of them are communicants. In its 90 schools are 7000 scholars, and last year its adherents were increased by 1228. Forty of its clergy are of African birth, and only seven are Europeans. Happily now a British Protectorate has been proclaimed over the Niger region, so that there is a fair prospect of uninterrupted labour. Twenty years ago the Niger was almost closed to the white man; now there is an export trade of two millions sterling annually, and a steady increase of Christians and Christian influence. Adverse influences, however, are at work. If Christian Missions are active, so are Mohammedans, and the number of converts they gain here, as well as elsewhere, are great. The vices, too, of white men are spreading among the natives.

Just to the south-east of these, there have been, for several years, Missions of the United Presbyterians at *Calabar*, the Baptists at *Cameroons*, the American Presbyterians on the *Gaboon*, and the Primitive Methodists at *Fernando Po*. The first of these for some years have laboured with much assiduity in Old Calabar, with no great amount of success. At 6 stations and 21 out-stations they have a variety of agents, consisting of 5 Scottish, 2 Jamaican, and 2 native ministers; 2 other European agents, 6 lady teachers, and 18 native assistants. The members in full communion are reported as 269, and the day scholars 517.

The Baptists have had a Mission for some time at Cameroons. The 5 stations and 5 out-stations have been under the charge of only 3 missionaries. The church members are 168, and the day scholars 540.

But a great change, not altogether auspicious, is beginning to affect Christian work here and on the opposite African coast. The whole of the Cameroons and Bimbia district, and the sea-board and interior, from Victoria to Old Calabar, has been annexed by Germany.

Southward of the river Campo, where German territory ends, to the Congo, for about 600 miles, and for an immense distance inland, France has taken possession. The Baptists have therefore transferred their Mission to the Basel Society, and the American Presbyterians, harrassed already by French interference, are reluctantly arranging, after more than forty years' toil, to give place to the Paris Society.

The Primitive Methodists at Fernando Po pay much attention to the 30,000 aboriginal Bubee race, and not in vain.

The American Presbyterian Missions at Gaboon and Corisco closely resemble the Baptist and United Presbyterian Missions in their neighbourhood, in native agency and results, though having a larger staff of male and female foreign agents.

South of these is the great valley of *The Congo* and its tributaries. It is estimated to cover 1,300,000 square miles, and to contain 40 million people. But no Mohammedan or Pagan government takes a census; the numbers given, therefore, are estimates only, and none, perhaps, are based on less information than those relating to the whole of Central Africa. Here three important Societies have recently established themselves, and the Missions had their origin in the discoveries of Livingstone and Stanley. The latter has proved that the Congo with its affluents is the true way into Central Africa from the West Coast, since it opens up 6000 miles of waterway through fertile and populous regions, affording the finest facilities for commerce, agriculture, and Christian enterprise.

The Livingstone Inland Mission sent its first two agents to Banana in 1878. Gradually, seven stations have been formed, five on the Lower, and two on the Upper Congo, and now the Mission is advancing far into the interior. Since 1884 it has passed, for its responsible management, from the hands of its founders, Mr. and Mrs. Grattan Guinness and their friends, to those of the American Baptist Missionary Union.

Fifty missionaries were sent out under the former management, of whom fourteen died, and several others had to return in broken health. But important pioneer work has been accomplished. The Gospel is made known through many districts, and, in some places, converts have been made. At Banza Mantaka there are more than one thousand native

Christians. At Palabala, also, the prospects are bright, and great care is said to prevail in the reception of converts. Two coloured missionaries from a freedmen's Missionary Association in America, have a station assigned them at Mukimvica; and some Swedish missionaries are similarly allied to the leading Society, whose missionaries number about 30. It works in at least four of the languages spoken on the river, and has translated the four gospels, portions of the history of the Old Testament, Peep of Day, and many of Sankey's hymns, which the people are fond of singing. Much medical work is also done among the people, two medical missionaries, Dr. Sims and Dr. Small, being connected with it.

The Baptist Missionary Society sent out its first agents in 1878. It has three stations on the lower and two on the upper immense reaches of the river; and with a large-hearted nobleness of purpose which deserves, and will doubtless command success, purposes to increase the latter to ten. Some schools have been formed; a few converts have been gathered; and about 20 missionaries are in the field. It is too early to speak of results, and unwise to anticipate, except in general terms, what the fortunes of the mission may be. Its sphere is immense. The "resources of European civilisation" will protect it from savage violence and Mohammedan fanaticism, save in isolated instances. In some places the missionaries are welcomed by the natives; but in others they are not. Portuguese and Arab slave dealers will attempt to thwart their benevolent aims; and the climate, which already has stricken down many missionaries, although now better understood, will strike down many more. Nevertheless it is a noble, interesting, and promising field. Who will not hope and pray that the triumphs won by the Society in Bengal and Jamaica may be more than equalled on the Congo?

Bishop Taylor of the American Methodist Episcopal Church, who has founded mixed and independent missions in Chili, Brazil, Liberia, and India, is now engaged in the arduous undertaking of leading a large party of men, women, and children to form self-supporting missions in the great basin of the Upper Congo. This vast region, lying to the west of the three great lakes, is untouched by any form of Christian agency, and we may well bid the energetic bishop God speed on his hazardous enterprise. He has set a noble example, much needed at a time when Missions are so expensively equipped, by walking at the head of his party, though past middle age, distances of 150 and 300 miles, and then expressing his intention "to start on equally extensive journeys." Already he has located a party of Friends to begin a mission of their own; also parties of his own people in Angola, on the south-west, at Kabinda, on the north, near the mouth of the great river, and at five stations inland from Loanda. His next purpose is to found a station at the south-east corner of Stanley Pool, and another on a point 400 miles above, at the junction of the great Sankuru and Kassai rivers, and to make these the basis for yet farther advances. A fourth contingent of artisan labourers is preparing to join him.

This vast field is not only intensely interesting, it is full of promise. It is healthier than the East or West Coasts. It can be reached with less trouble, expense, and danger, than can the interior from any other direction. It has not been injured as a Mission field, as North Africa has, by Mohammedan intolerance, nor as the South, by war and aggression.

In *Benguela* an attempt was made, in 1880, by the American Board of Commissioners to begin an important group of missions. After a promising beginning at Bailundu, 250 miles from the Coast, reverse came, in part by the characteristic falseness of a Portuguese liquor seller, whose slanders were not met by adequate courage and wisdom. The work was resumed in 1884, and now at Bailundu, Bihe, and Benguela town, five missionaries and five female missionaries have a fine field before them.

SOUTH AFRICA

May be generally described as including all territory south of Benguela, on the West Coast, and the Zambesi on the East. The population is from five to six millions, and differs considerably from that of the negro type predominant on the West Coast. The Kaffirs, or Bantus, are the most numerous, varied, and intelligent of the native races, and are supposed to number three millions. Next to these are the Hottentots, and lower still, the degraded Bushmen. Negroes, Arabs, and half castes are numerous, whilst the European population, amounting to not less than 330,000, is almost entirely Dutch and English. The former settled at the Cape in the middle of the sixteenth century; but the first to care for the natives was George Schmidt, a Moravian, who settled among the *Hottentots* at Gradenthal, in 1737. He was successful, but was driven home by his own countrymen, and the Mission was only resumed in 1792 by three artisans. Gradually, other settlements were formed. In 1822 there were six, with a total Christian population of 5300; but the hopes of progress and permanence then cherished have not been realised.

The London Missionary Society was second in the field. In 1798, it sent out the renowned Dr. Vanderkemp and three other missionaries. Two of these settled among the *Bushmen* of the colony, but Vanderkemp went to *Kaffraria*. Since then, this Society has taken a prominent part in South African evangelisation, and has been represented by able men, of whom Philip, Livingstone, and Moffat are the best known. But its missions have not grown and prospered as might have been anticipated, and are now found only in *Kafirland*, *Bechuanaland*, and among the *Matebele*. The native adherents are 9000. Several Christian communities, however, throughout South Africa, now independent, owe their origin to this Society, some of which, at too early a stage, were cast by it on their own insufficient resources.

The Wesleyans entered South Africa in 1814. They have given much attention to the European colonists, and in *Cape Colony, Natal,* and the other Colonies comprising South Africa, have more than 1300 preaching places, 23,000 accredited members, an aggregate attendance on public worship of 101,000, and 15,000 scholars in their schools.

The Presbyterian Missions originated with the Glasgow Society, which in 1823 sent its first agent. They now belong to the Free and United Presbyterian Churches, and have their principal stations in *Kaffraria.* Both are flourishing in various directions. The latter at 10 principal stations has a rapidly growing body of 2180 communicants; the former, in 29 churches, has 3170 communicants, and 3500 scholars in its schools. The well-known and most useful Lovedale Institution for the training of preachers, teachers, and artisans, belongs to the Free Church, whilst with the liberality which distinguishes its many Missions, its advantages, and even its professorships, are open to all. It has also three stations in Natal, where the results are similar, though less.

The Rhenish Missionary Society commenced in 1828, and has now a chain of fine stations stretching along the West Coast from Cape Colony, through *Namaqualand, Damara,* and *Ovampo,* a distance of almost 1000 miles. Attached to these are at least 15,000 adherents.

The Paris Missionary Society sent its first agents in 1829. They eventually settled among the *Basutos,* and have now extended their labours to the *Zambesi.* The Boers have repeatedly impeded them; nevertheless they have been highly successful, and have now more than 20,000 Basuto converts and 3000 scholars.

The missions of the Berlin Society in *Cape Colony,*

Kaffraria, Natal, the *Transvaal*, and *Orange Free State*, took their rise in 1834; those of the American Board in Natal in 1833; of the Propagation Society in 1833; of the Dutch in 1842; of the Norwegians among the *Zulus* in 1842; of the Hermannsberg Society in Natal, the Transvaal, and Zululand in 1856; finally came the Free Church of the Canton de Vaud, which has two small stations in the Transvaal— altogether fifteen missions, the native adherents of which number almost 200,000.

South Africa is thus better supplied with Mission agencies than any region of similar extent and populousness.

EAST AFRICA

Has fewer and smaller Missions than are to be found along the West Coast, but the Zulu war, and an idea for some time prevalent that the Central regions of the Continent could best be entered from the East, has led to the establishment of some new Missions.

Some of the older Societies in the South have now their stations among the Zulus, and some that are altogether new have been formed.

The American Board has adopted the 500 miles of coast between *Limpopo and the Zambesi* as its field. Already missionaries are located in three different positions, and from these it is intended to penetrate into the interior.

The intrepid M. Coillard has long desired to extend the French Mission of Basutoland eastward, and recently, in spite of great difficulties, mainly arising from tribal feuds, reached the upper waters of the Zambesi, where he has been welcomed by the chiefs and people. Two Basuto evangelists, a medical missionary and five or six others, are now with M. Coillard at Mombara and Sesheke, and hope soon to locate some of their number at Lialui, the capital. The country is more than 800 miles in length, and populous.

More than five years ago, a young Scotchman named

Arnot, filled with a desire to explore Africa and evangelise some portion of it, set out, apparently with very inadequate resources of any kind. Landing in Natal, he gradually found his way into the Orange Free State, then to Shoshong, where he confirmed all that has been said of the Christian character of its chief, Kama; then appeared among the Barotse, on the upper reaches of the Zambesi; then, suddenly, at Bihe and Bailundu, on the West Coast; and, finally, last year, went back north-eastward to Garenganze, where the country is "full of people," and his "prospects are beyond his fondest expectations." We hope Mr. Arnot has now found a sphere where he will abide.

On the shores of *Lake Nyassa* the Presbyterians are active, and the English Universities' Mission have a station, which is intended to be one of a series, extending to Zanzibar. There the Mission is now based, with twelve missionaries, and as many native assistants. Originally it was designed to make the Zambesi its field of operations and its centre, and with this design Bishop Mackenzie, with six Englishmen and five coloured men from the south, reached there in 1861. The bishop, unfortunately, became involved in the tribal disputes of the natives. He and several of his party died, and within little more than a year the mission was at an end.

The Church of Scotland has had a station on Nyassa, at Blantyre, since 1874, and one at Damasi since 1884. The Missions are educational, evangelistic, medical, and industrial, under the charge of ten European agents, who have suffered less from the climate than those of any African Mission recently formed. Native weakness and tribal quarrels have impeded and threatened the Mission, but its prospects are brighter than they were.

Here also, on the western and southern sides of the lake, the Free Church have five stations and a considerable staff of agents engaged in very various pursuits.

The Church Missionary Society formed a station on the East Coast at *Mombasa* as far back as 1844, and within the last ten years it has formed several others on the way both to the south and north sides of the *Victoria Nyanza*. About 200 miles from the Coast, opposite Zanzibar, on the southern route to the lake, it has three stations, in Usagara. More than 300 miles westward, it has another at Uvui, and one at Msalala, at the southern end of the lake. Then, north of Zanzibar, on the Coast, near Mombasa, it has four stations; another, direct inland 90 miles, at Teita; another, 50 miles yet farther inland near the famed mountain Kilima-njaro; and, since 1877, its farthest outpost has been at Rubaga, in *Uganda*, on the northern side of Nyanza.

In leaving the Coast and penetrating into the interior, the Mission has had to contend with enormous difficulties, involving danger, delay, and expense. The natives are exacting and suspicious;* the Arab traders are influential and unfriendly; the climate is treacherous; and the European powers, by their earth-hunger, have deepened the distrust alike of chiefs and people. Some of the missionaries have died, others have had to return, and from one cause or another, the work has been retarded. Bishop Hannington's murder, and the frightful sufferings even unto death of several baptised Christians in Uganda, attest the efficiency of the workers and the success of their work; but, among a people intensely ignorant, cruel, suspicious; affected, and not without occasion, by rumours of European invasion; influenced by Arabs, who, as traders,

---

* "I have little doubt that the history of a Mission here,—at Mandara, —if properly maintained, would be the counterpart of most of our Missions,—the reception of the white man with joy and gladness, everything done for him for a week or two; then a cooling down of the first love, neglect, perhaps even persecution; after which, if patiently endured, fresh overtures, a mutual understanding, deepening into confidence and love; then a gradual opening of the door, a breaking down of superstitions, a reception of the sweet Gospel of peace of the Saviour of mankind."—Bishop HANNINGTON.

slave-dealers, and Mohammedans, hate our presence; led by chiefs cruel and heartless, as the one who murdered Bishop Hannington; and governed by a monarch such as he who now rules over Uganda, it is impossible to divine what may occur. So uncertain and critical a state of affairs calls for and encourages prayer, that God would be pleased to move the minds of some according to His will, and thwart the purposes of those who devise mischief in their hearts against His cause and people.

But there are numerous signs, even in Uganda, that the seed of the kingdom has taken root. Many wish for instruction. Religious services are numerously attended. Some persons of rank and many of the people profess faith in Christ, and not a few of them have the courage of their convictions, although to sympathise with the missionary is to be marked and suspected.

In the 11 stations of this important Mission, there are 25 European missionaries, 2 native clergymen, and 21 native lay teachers. The baptised adherents number 745, and the unbaptised, 1459. The communicants are 246, and the scholars, 554.

In 1877 the London Missionary Society resolved to occupy the third and most western of the great lakes, *Tanganyika*. Repeated contingents of men, in some instances of much experience, like South African missionaries, and the late lamented secretary of the Society, Dr. Mullens, have been sent, only to die or to be driven back by disease or apprehension. The climate, and the long, trying journey from Zanzibar, not always wisely arranged, have proved very disastrous, nevertheless, two stations have been formed—one at Urambo, a few stages east of the lake, another on Kavala Island, near its western shore, where the strength of the enterprise is concentrated. A third station at its southern extremity has been projected, but is not now occupied.

Unhealthy as much of Equatorial Africa undoubtedly is,

there are localities in it that are more happily placed. The country around Kilima-njaro seems of this nature. Dr. Thompson, the traveller, and Bishop Hannington, have spoken of it in the highest terms. There the American Presbyterians purpose to found a mission.

Dr. Krapf, of the Church Missionary Society, was the first to call public attention to the little-known region lying southeast of Abyssinia. In 1844 he began his labours there, and as a missionary, an explorer, and a writer, did more than any one previous to Livingstone to call attention to North-Eastern and Central Africa. Right across the Dark Continent—from north of the Senegal on the west, to the Somali country—is that vast zone of country, vaguely called the Great Desert and the Soudan, to which we have before alluded. It is more destitute of Christian agency than any region of similar extent, not even excepting Central Asia. But it contains no countries to which any considerable number of missionaries should at present be sent, when their services are likely elsewhere to meet with so much more satisfactory results. The presence of Mohammedanism, of slavery in its worst forms, of despotism, the greed and jealousy of rival chiefs, and the lawless, unsettled state of the various races, are most unfavourable to steady Christian effort.

Among the *Galla tribes*, east of this dark region, some attempts have been made to plant Christian truth. Missionaries of the Chrischona Society labour here; and among the same people, at Ribe and Jomva, the United Methodists have missionaries, who have met with some success. Recently, a praiseworthy attempt to extend their Mission has, for the present, met with disaster. In 1885, Mr. and Mrs. Houghton went to establish a station north of the two we have named, and last year were cruelly killed by those they so disinterestedly sought to benefit.

Abyssinia is not a promising sphere. From 1829, when Gobat and Kugler were sent there by the Church Missionary

Society, repeated attempts have been made to evangelise it, and with no encouraging results. At present only the Chrischona Pilgrims and the Lunds Society (Swedish) have small missions among its three million people.

At *Zanzibar* the University's Mission is in some strength, and exerting considerable influence on the adjoining mainland, and on the classes who trade with the interior. Also at the *Seychelles* and the *Mauritius* small Episcopal Missions are found.

MADAGASCAR,

As the only African island of considerable size, and on account of its extraordinary Christian history, is worthy of extended notice. The first two missionaries were sent by the London Missionary Society in 1818. So little was known of the climate and the seasons that in a few weeks one of them, both their wives, and their two children died. The solitary survivor retired to the Mauritius, but in 1820 returned with a coadjutor, and settled in the capital, being well received by the king. Joined by four or five others, schools were established, the Scriptures were translated, and some useful arts introduced.

But the death of King Radama, in 1828, clouded the fair prospect. Gradually a reactionary policy was adopted. Baptism, first of the soldiers, then of any, was prohibited. The schools were closed, worship was forbidden, and the missionaries sent away. Fines, imprisonment, slavery, death, were the penalties inflicted on hundreds, if not thousands, during 25 years. When the missionaries ultimately left in 1836, 30,000 scholars had been in their schools, and numbers had some acquaintance with Christian truth, but less than 200 had avowed their faith by baptism.

But the dark cloud passed away when Queen Ranavalona died in 1860, and many thousands then avowed themselves Christians. The London Missionary Society at once sent missionaries, who were so eagerly welcomed, that their number has been repeatedly reinforced, and they have been favoured to witness results only equalled once or twice in modern times. How the work has grown cannot now be described, but more than 1200 congregations meet every Sabbath for Christian worship. The professing Christians associated with this one Society are 230,400, but a far greater number express their sympathy with Christianity. The church members are 61,723; the native preachers, 4395, besides 828 who rank, through training or efficiency, as ministers, and who instruct the Christians and evangelise the heathen; whilst in 1043 schools 97,891 pupils are taught. The whole is under the superintendence of 27 European male and 4 female missionaries.

These figures express remarkable results, and they are not all. The self-denial and zeal of multitudes is undoubted. An immense amount of Christian work is done gratuitously. The 900 churches in the province of Imerina are almost all self-supporting. In the last 15 years they have built, and paid for, more than 700 places of worship, many of them large, and expressive of growing taste. They have formed a home mission, and orphan, and other Societies, evidential of consolidation, self-reliance, and zeal, and they contribute annually between £4000 and £5000 to Christian uses. A normal school, a college for the training of evangelists and ministers, and a good printing establishment, add greatly to the efficiency of the Mission. Three other Societies have missions on the island.

The Friends Foreign Missions Association is represented by 19 missionaries, including ladies, who work in great harmony with the London Society. They have in charge 125 stations, and are assisted by 319 native preachers. Even on their strict principles, they have 3133 members. Their schools contain more than 14,000 scholars, and in 1885 their printing press issued 68,000 publications.

The first missionaries of the Norwegian (Lutheran) Society

arrived in 1867, and settled among the Betsileo. Among them they chiefly labour, though they have stations also among the Sakalavas, and a representative mission in the capital. Since 1881 their progress has been great, and now they have more than 220 places of worship, to which are attached 38,000 adherents, of whom more than 5000 are communicants. In their schools are 35,000 scholars. The whole, including a printing press and a seminary for teachers, is under the charge of from 20 to 30 missionaries.

The Propagation Society commenced in 1864. Its spheres are the capital, Tamatave, and among the Betsimisaraka. Its 10 European missionaries are aided by 3 ladies, some ordained native ministers, and 87 catechists. The number of its adherents and scholars are considerably less than those of the Norwegian Society.

CHAPTER VIII.

MISSION FIELDS AND AGENCIES—ASIA AND POLYNESIA.

E now turn to Asia, the teeming population of which exceeds that of Europe, Africa, and America combined. The only country of Asia in which Christianity predominates is

ASIATIC RUSSIA,

and there, among its scattered and benighted population, the need of the true evangelist is great.

TURKEY,

including the almost independent European Provinces, and Egypt, has a population thus religiously distributed:—

Creed.	Europe.	Asia.	Africa.	Total.
Mohammedan,	5,900,000	12,870,000	3,800,000	22,570,000
Greek Church,	9,480,000	2,360,000	700,000	12,840,000
Armenian,	300,000			
Roman Catholic, &c.,	450,000	640,000		1,090,000
Jewish,	70,000	150,000	300,000	520,000
Druse, &c.,		80,000		80,000
Total,	16,200,000	16,100,000	4,800,000	37,100,000

Throughout the empire, the obstacles in the way of Christian evangelisation are great, for it is questionable if anywhere the life of a convert from Islam would be safe; and the influence of the ruling classes is as intensely though quietly hostile to Christianity as it well can be. Three features of its Missions are—that they are principally American, are educational, and are directed toward the nominally Christian population.

In *European Turkey*, the American Board has five stations and thirty-one missionaries. Its centre is the Robert College, Constantinople—the most important and liberalising institution in the empire. Among its students are many young men of position from Greece, Bulgaria, Servia, and Macedonia. In Constantinople are also small Missions of the Friends, the American Episcopal Methodists, two agents of the Bible Society, and a large staff of American lady workers, with a smaller agency from the Society for Promoting Female Education in the East. The Free Church of Scotland has here an important Mission to the Jews. Education, literature, and medicine are the principal channels through which these various agencies act, and with great effect, in breaking down prejudice and diffusing true Christian ideas; but with the smallest results in converts from Islam.

In *Asiatic Turkey*, especially in Syria and Palestine, the agencies are more varied. The American Board has 70 agents in 16 stations—some of them, at Erzeroum, Trebizond, and Harpoot, being of considerable importance. Altogether, it has throughout the empire nearly 100 evangelical churches, principally self-supported and self-directed.

Next in strength comes the Foreign Mission Board of the Presbyterian Church of the United States, with fourteen missions. Its headquarters are at Beirut, where, in the midst of its 80,000 inhabitants, it has the Syrian Protestant College and an important printing establishment; the former a fine centre of general education and of medical and theological training; the latter for the production of Christian literature, especially in Arabic, which carries the Gospel message into regions in Arabia and Africa where the missionary cannot penetrate. It has also stations at Abieh, Sidon, Tripoli, and Zahleh. Medicine and schools are important factors in the work done; and in spite of the difficulties arising out of Turkish misrule, the missions are efficient and progressive. The converts and schools contribute well to the funds. The Irish and the American United Presbyterians labour in Syria, and at Aintab there is a theological and medical college.

The Lebanon is not neglected. The Free Church of Scotland is active around Shweir, and its training school supplies teachers to many villages around. Schools sustained by Anglo-American Friends and some Ladies' Societies in Britain, who make Syria their special care, stretch right across the Lebanon from Syria to Damascus. Altogether, the converts in Syria who have been won from the decayed Churches of the East to evangelical Protestantism number 30,000, and the scholars in the schools to 12,000.

Palestine, with a very mixed population of less than one million, has received much attention, but as a mission field it has disappointed many hopes.

The Church Missionary Society sent Mr. Jowett, its first agent, as early as 1815, and Dr. Gobat, another of its missionaries, was from 1846, for thirty years, the first Bishop of Jerusalem. It has now six missionaries—at Jerusalem, Nazareth, El Salt, Nablus, Jaffna, and Gaza — who superintend a considerable amount of evangelistic and educational work in these districts. Their converts do not number 1800, nor their scholars 2000.

As early as 1820 the American Board sent missionaries who settled at Jerusalem, but attempted to found missions also at Jaffa and Beirut. Others followed, but in 1843, after the death of twenty missionaries, and very inadequate results, the spheres were abandoned in favour of Syria.

Scotch medical missionaries labour at Nazareth and Tiberias, and Dr. Avedis Yeretsian, an Armenian, trained in America, and now settled at Cesarea, is reported to have excited a great spirit of inquiry among the people. At Nablus there is a small Baptist Society; at Jaffna a medical mission and some superior schools, not connected with the Society mentioned. The German colony at Haifa is exerting similar considerable influence on the population around, and their good schools are open to all. Finally, some ladies are active as independent agents, or as representatives of European or American Societies.

Armenia has had the occasional services only of some American missionaries, but since 1885 Baptist agents from the New World have been established there.

Arabia has no missionary history. From Syria and Egypt attempts have been made to reach the large adjoining Arab population, and to spread the Gospel eastward. The results have not been encouraging. Fresh attempts are now being made. The recently-formed Society for the Berber races of North Africa and the Church Missionary Society desire to enter the country. General Haig has recently reported unfavourably of attempts wherever Turkish power prevails, but thinks more hopefully of independent Arabia. Keith Falconer's attempt has already been described.

Persia

Has a population of about 4,400,000 which, with the exception of less than a quarter of a million, is Mohammedan. Various attempts have been made to convert the people, but no marked results have followed. Those have principally emanated from America. It is unnecessary to refer to some romantic attempts to plant the Gospel here, made during last century and the beginning of this by the Moravians, by Henry Martyn, Mr. Groves, and Professor Newman. The more recent efforts date from 1833, when the American Board founded a station at Oroomiah, among the Nestorians, which, after many changes, was transferred to the American Presbyterian Board about sixteen years ago. It has a western group of stations whose centre is Oroomiah, and an eastern one at Teheran and Hamadan, though 200 miles apart. In both groups medical, educational, and preaching agencies are combined, and with considerable results. There is general encouragement over all the field. At the 5 stations there are 30 churches, having 2000 communicants. The native ministers are numerous; the people give to the mission £500 annually; the schools are 115, and the scholars 2730.

The Church Missionary Society has had a station at Julfa, near Ispahan, since 1876, and more recently has formed another at Baghdad. Connected with the former is a native church, under a native pastor, several schools, one of them industrial, an orphanage, a medical mission, and a Bible and book depôt. Five European missionaries are at the two stations. Every one familiar with Bible lands must feel deeply interested in the fortunes of a mission formed at Baghdad.

CENTRAL ASIA

Is without missionaries. Regretful as this may be, we cannot see how it can wisely be otherwise. Too frequently missionaries are sent where there are none, with little regard to adverse circumstances; whilst open and promising fields, because they already have a few, though a most inadequate number, are neglected. Money and human lives have often thus been misapplied—wasted. It would be a waste of both to send agents into this vast, wild, misgoverned, and most fanatical region. No missionary's life would be safe if he really did that for which he was sent. The probability of making a single convert would be remote, whilst it is certain the life of no convert would be safe. All that can be done is by out-posts, such as are furnished by the Persian, Syrian, Kashmere, and Peshawur Missions, which may reach individuals from Affghanistan and the countries in question, and send into them Christian books.

INDIA,

Through English magnanimity, presents a far different spectacle. It is peaceful, progressive, prosperous beyond any non-Christian country, and in spite of the wide diversity it presents of nationality, language, civilisation, and religion, missionary labour in its various forms is carried on with less interruption than in any non-Christian land. Its immense population is religiously thus divided—

Hindus,	190,931,450
Mohammedans,	51,127,585
*Idolators, other than Hindus,	6,426,511
Sikhs,	853,426
†Buddhists,	6,250,000
Jains, Parsees, Jews,	229,135
Roman Catholic natives,	865,643
Protestant natives,	417,372
Syrian Christians,	300,000
‡Europeans and Eurasians	204,000

It is unnecessary here to enter further into the history of Protestant Missions, than to remark that though they date from 1706, there were not more than 50 missionaries sent out all through last century, nor more than 10 at work at any one time. Even during the first third of this century, up to 1833, when the East India Company's Charter was renewed and liberalised, the number of missionaries did not average 150, nor the ordained native ministers 10, whilst other agents were as limited. For some years after the commencement of the century only six Societies were at work. It will be seen, therefore, from the following statements how greatly the agencies and their results have increased. These figures do not include Burmah or Ceylon :—

* Belonging to the aboriginal hill tribes.
† All in Burmah.
‡ Including the European army of about 70,000.

Missionary Societies,	47
Isolated or personal Missions,	7
Foreign missionaries,	586
Foreign lay helpers,	72
Foreign male teachers,	98
Foreign female teachers,	479
Ordained native ministers,	461
Native preachers,	2488
Native Christian male teachers,	1643
Native Christian female teachers,	2462
Non-Christian male teachers,	2462
Non-Christian female teachers,	281
Stations,	569
Churches or congregations,	3650
Native communicants,	113,325
Native Christians,	417,372

The following is a list of the Societies having Missions in India, with their principal spheres. We have not thought it necessary to indicate the spheres of those Societies which are the largest, and which are to be found in several of the Provinces of India :—

1. BAPTIST SOCIETIES :

American Baptist Missionary Union—Telingana, Assam, Cooch Behar.
American Free Will Baptist Missionary Union— North Orissa.
Baptist Missionary Society—Bengal, North-West Provinces.
General Baptist Missionary Society—Orissa, Gangam, Sumbulpur.
Canadian Baptist Missionary Society—Telingana.
South Australian Baptist Missionary Society—Eastern Bengal.

MISSION FIELDS AND AGENCIES—ASIA AND POLYNESIA.   107

2. CHURCH OF ENGLAND:
   Society for the Propagation of the Gospel.
   Church Missionary Society.
   Oxford Brotherhood of St. Paul—Calcutta.
   Cambridge University Mission—Delhi.
   Scottish Episcopal Church—Chunda.

3. CONGREGATIONAL:
   American Board of Commissioners—Bombay, Satara, Sholapur, Madura.
   London Missionary Society.

4. BASEL MISSIONARY SOCIETY:
   Dharwar, North and South Canara, Malabar Coast, Nilgiris.

5. LUTHERAN:
   American Lutheran Missionary Society—Kistna and Godavery Districts.
   Danish Lutheran Missionary Society—Arcot Province.
   Gossner's Missionary Society—Behar, Chota Nagpur.
   Leipsic Lutheran Missionary Society — Tranquebar, Tanjore, Bangalore, Trichinopoly, Madras.
   Hermannsberg Missionary Society—Nellore.
   Swedish Evangelical Lutheran Missionary Society—Central Provinces.

6. METHODIST:
   American Episcopal Methodist Missionary Society.
   American Free Will Methodist Missionary Society—Central Provinces.
   Wesleyan Methodist Missionary Society—Mysore, Coimbatur, Bengal.
   Welsh Calvinistic Methodist Missionary Society—Assam.

7. PRESBYTERIAN:
   Church of Scotland—Calcutta, Punjab, Darjeeling, Independent Sikhim.

Free Church of Scotland—Calcutta, Bombay, Poona, Madras, Nagpur, Santhalisthan.

United Presbyterian Church of Scotland—Rajputana.

Presbyterian Church in England—Rampore, Banleah, in Bengal.

Presbyterian Church of Ireland—Gujerat.

Original Secession Synod of Scotland—Seoni, in Central Provinces.

Presbyterian Church of the United States of America—Bengal, North-West Provinces, Punjab, Gwalior.

United Presbyterian Church of the United States of America—North-West Provinces, Punjab.

Reformed (Dutch) Church of America—Arcot, North and South.

Basel Missionary Society of the United States of America—Central Provinces and Tinnevelly.

Canadian Presbyterians—Indore.

8. FRIENDS:
   Friends' Mission—Hosungabad, in Central Provinces.

9. SALVATION ARMY:
   South India.

There are also small independent Missions at Calcutta, Gopalgunge, in Bengal, Ellichpur, and Chikalda in the Central Provinces, in the north and south of South Berar,* at Narsapur on the Godavery, Colar in Mysore, and in Santhalisthan.

Noble work is done in a most Christian and heroic manner in some, if not all these independent missions. Miss Reade,

---

* Berar has an area of 17,711 square miles, and a population of 2,672,673 souls, almost equal to that of Ceylon; yet its Christian agencies consist only of one native Free Church pastor at Amraoti; another connected with the Church Missionary Society at Boldana; a small "faith" Mission in charge of three agents at Bassim; another with, at the most, three male missionaries, and some female assistance at Ellichpur.

for instance, in South Arcot, is toiling with no European coadjutor, and imperfect native help, to care for orphans, to restore the sick, to visit and instruct women, and to preach the Gospel publicly in the villages of the large district in which she resides. So also pathos, romance, and benevolence characterise in an unusual degree the work of Miss Anstey, at Kolar, near Bangalore. Since 1877 she has been there a light in a dark place. With but slight personal resources, and unsustained by any Society, she began a work which has grown in blessed influence. At one time she had in charge 800 children, mostly orphans, an orphanage, a Christian band of some 170 members, two Christian villages, together with artisan and industrial work; and the respect and admiration of the heathen around attest how real and beneficent the work is.

Several of the larger Societies have now important Ladies' Associations connected with them; and others, not identified with any particular Mission, are of great value, such as the Society for Promoting Female Education in the East, and the American Women's Union Zenana Mission.

Other auxiliary agencies are of great value, as the Bible, the Tract, the Christian Book Societies, the Christian Vernacular Educational Society, and the Medical Missionary Society.

Burmah

Has a population computed at 6,747,000. Missionary effort has hitherto been practically confined to what, until last year, was called British Burmah and Mandalay.

The American Baptist Union has taken the lead in this interesting field. Judson was the first of its missionaries in 1813, though a Mission was begun a few years earlier, by the noble band at Serampore. Since 1859 small missions have been established by the Society for the Propagation of the Gospel at Rangoon, Maulmain, Taunghoo, and Mandalay; more recently at Rangoon, by the American Episcopal Methodists, and at the Andaman Islands, by the Church Misssionary Society.

The first-named Society is distinguished for its early romantic history, its striking success among the Karen tribes, and the praiseworthy efforts of the missionaries in Bassim to make their missions self-supporting.* The relative strength of this and the other Societies will be seen in the following table :—

American Baptist Union.

Missionaries.	Ordained Native Ministers.	Native Preachers.	Congregations.	Native Christians.	Communicants.
29	108	304	472	70,094	23,928

Other Societies.

Missionaries.	Ordained Native Ministers.	Native Preachers.	Congregations.	Native Christians.	Communicants.
7	6	64	57	5,416	1,001

Under British rule all Burmah will become an open and most promising field for the propagation of the Gospel.

Ceylon

Has a population of 2,850,000, religiously thus distributed—

Buddhists,	1,960,000
Hindus,	465,944
Mohammedans,	172,000
Christians,	252,056
	2,850,000

The suggestive and disappointing early history of Christianity on the island has already been described. Nor have

---

* "Self-support in Bassim," by C. H. Carpenter, Boston, U.S.A.

the past seventy years of effort yielded all the results that might fairly have been anticipated. The population being largely Buddhist, is more approachable than are Hindus or Mohammedans. The island has been blessed with peace and good government, and the missionaries have had a free and open field. But the ill savour of the past, the apathy of the Cingalese character, and the indifference induced by Buddhism to all earnest, self-denying, and dogmatic doctrine and practice, such as true Christianity demands, may in part explain this comparative failure.

The present agencies were begun as follows—

Baptist Missionary Society,	1813
Wesleyan Missionary Society,	1814
American Board,	1816
Church Missionary Society,	1818
Gospel Propagation Society,	1824

The total number of foreign missionaries is 36, one half of them being Wesleyans. The total number of converts is not large, being only 35,708, the scholars number 30,531. Four-fifths of the former belong to the Propagation and Wesleyan Societies.

SIAM

Is little more than a geographical expression to Englishmen, though it has features of great interest. Its population, supposed to number six or eight millions, is almost entirely Buddhist.

Three American Societies have in Siam small missions, which are largely medical and educational. A Baptist mission dates from 1833, and two Presbyterian ones from 1848. Their success is limited, but the field is opening, and the marked favour shown in recent years by the Government to the missions has continued, and has recently had some notable manifestations.

Laos

is less known even than other provinces of Siam. 500 miles north of Bankok, where the American Presbyterian Board labour, they have had a mission since 1867. At two stations, six missionaries are engaged in medical, educational, and evangelistic work, but with small success.

West of Laos in Northern Siam, among the Karens, the Baptists commenced a Mission in 1882, which promises to be as successful and self-propagating as that in Burmah among the same race. It has already formed three churches, which have a membership of 160.

Cambodia,

formerly a powerful empire, but which has been greatly reduced by the aggressions of its Siamese and Annamite neighbours, is without any Protestant missionaries.

Annam

is religiously in the same unhappy position, though Roman Catholicism has been here from the time of Xavier, and is said to have 400,000 adherents. The empire includes, or rather did before the last unjust interference of the French, the rich and populous province or kingdom of Tongking to the north, Annam and Cochin China in the centre, and French Cochin China to the south; a splendid territory, covering an area greater than Britain and Ireland, stretching along the China Sea for a thousand miles, and with a population variously estimated at 10,500,000 and 14,000,000.

Through the interference of the French in Annamese affairs, a deep sentiment of hostility to white men and Christianity has possessed the people, from which the native Roman Catholics, "protected" by the French, have been the first to suffer. It is reported on good authority, that in July and August 1885, 30,000 Christians in one district, out of 41,000, were massacred. From five to twelve European priests were killed. Two seminaries, an orphanage, 12 convents of native nuns, 200 places of worship, and almost all the houses of the Christians were pillaged and burned.

China,

Like India, demands far more attention than can here be given to it. Its enormous area of 5,300,000 square miles, whilst Great Britain and Ireland contain only 120,000 square miles, and its teeming population, which numbers at least 300,000,000, are ample evidence of its immense importance as a Mission field.

The London Missionary Society has the honour of having sent the first Protestant missionary in 1807, and ever since it has been represented by one or more of the most scholarly and able of the missionaries in China. Morrison, Milne, Medhurst, Legge, Edkins, and John have been among its representatives.

In 1830 the great empire became more open to Christian effort, when the American Board, followed in 1837 by the Church Missionary Society, entered on the field. Since then the increase alike in Societies and missionaries has been great; so that now 16 British Societies, having 241 missionaries, 13 American ones with 214, and 4 Continental ones with 25, are there represented. The three Societies named above, and the China Inland Mission, have the largest number of missionaries. The latter alone has 182, and hopes soon to increase the number.

It is obvious that the agency is inadequate. And it will appear the more so if it be considered, that the proportion of native agents to foreign missionaries is far less than in most Mission fields; for it is remarkable that whilst in India, Polynesia, and Madagascar, native agents are numerous, it is otherwise in Africa and China. There are, therefore, provinces containing respectively 5, 7, 8, 15, and 18 million people, in which there is not a resident missionary to each million of the population. Preaching tours, made very occasionally in such provinces, however important, are obviously not all that they should have.

It was not till 1842 that China was really open to Christian effort, and since then the progress made has been steady, though not great. When the first missionary—Dr. Morrison—died in 1834, there were 6 missionaries only among the Chinese residents of the Straits of Malacca, and 7 converts. In China proper, there was no missionary and no convert, for the profession of Christianity was a capital offence.

Beside China proper, there are its four outlying dependencies of *Manchuria, Mongolia, Sungaria,* and *Thibet;* the first and the last supposed to contain 8 million population each, the others 5 and 2 millions.

Missionaries would not be permitted to reside in some of these countries; and in others they could do but little if they were there. Therefore, occasional visits into Mongolia from Peking, by Mr. Gilmour, of the London Society's Mission, and into Thibet by the two solitary Moravians at Poo and Kailung in the Himalayas, or in the very limited sphere which is sure to be allotted by the jealousy of the Government, to one of the Moravians, who has received permission to reside at Leh, the capital of Middle Thibet, are illustrations of what alone can be done. Only in one or two instances do missionaries reside in the territories named. Thus Mr. Shaw, of the Irish Presbyterian Society, and Mr. Ross and Mr. Webster, of the United Presbyterians, at Moukden in Manchuria, keep a watchful eye on the regions beyond. The latter speaks of "fully 600 believers openly professing their faith," and a yet greater number of secret disciples, as well as a wide diffusion of Christian knowledge.

But the religious apathy and the intellectual latitudinarianism induced by Buddhism, together with race complacency and immobility, and dread and dislike of Europeans

—strengthened, alas! by our opium policy, our wars, and French intrusiveness—have impeded Missions all over the empire.

Corea,

Though two and a-half times as large as Scotland, and estimated to contain 15 million people, has, until recently, been without the Gospel. Now the dawn of a better time seems perceptible. The instructions of the missionaries last-mentioned, and of the agents of the Bible Society, have reached the hearts of many Coreans, who have sought refuge in Manchuria from the troubles afflicting their own country, and who desire to convey to it their new-found faith. Already about 100 have been baptised, and in Corea itself many seem to desire the Gospel.

Corea is also being entered from another direction, and in an interesting manner. Two Chinese, who are to be entirely supported by the converts at Foochow, have recently been sent to labour in it, a well-to-do Chinaman having contributed £200 wherewith to begin the Mission.

Formosa,

With 3,000,000 population, has 3 ordained, 2 medical, 1 teaching, and 2 lady missionaries of the English Presbyterian, and 2 of the Canadian Presbyterian Church. These latter have in charge, in the north of the island, 34 stations; and though the work has been greatly hindered by recent war, the success on the whole has been considerable. Recently upwards of 2000 people expressed a desire to follow the Lord of Hosts, and hundreds have been baptised. The English Presbyterian Mission in the south has 34 stations.

The Pascadore Islands lie south-west of Formosa. From the latter to the former two native preachers have recently been sent by the native church connected with the English Presbyterian Mission. They have been well received by the people.

HAINAN,

The only other island of importance belonging to China, has a population of 1,000,000 Chinese, and an aboriginal independent population probably amounting to half-a-million. The first Christian labourer was Mr. C. C. Jeremiassen, who, after long service in the Chinese maritime customs, devoted himself in 1881 to medical and Christian work at Hoikou. A missionary from the mainland, who recently made a tour with this worthy man, writes: "I can say with emphasis that the whole country seems wonderfully open to Christian work. In ten years' work, extending over the greater part of the province of Canton, I never met with as much friendliness and genuine hospitality, as among these people." The Mission in 1886 was adopted and reinforced by the American Presbyterian Board.

JAPAN

Is almost as large as France and more populous than Great Britain and Ireland. As recently as 1859, the first Protestant missionaries reached it; but, through the dread and dislike of Christianity, which has been engendered by the political intrigues of the Roman Catholic missionaries in the seventeenth century, it was not until 1872 that publicity of Christian speech was allowed in the country.

Now 21 Societies have agents in the empire, 13 of them, with the greater number of missionaries, being American. The most important are the American Board, the American Protestant Episcopal Church, and the Church Missionary Society. The missionaries of some Presbyterian Societies have wisely united in one indigenous Presbyterian Church— an example which, with great advantage, might be followed in many places by others, as well as Presbyterians. The whole of the missionaries number about 150.

The progress made in Japan by Christianity during late years has been remarkable. There are already 93 native ministers and twice as many evangelists. The Churches formed number 103, and of those 64 are self-supporting. The membership is at least 15,000. Christian ideas and Western civilisation are spreading as in no Asiatic country, not excepting India, and nowhere are the fields whiter for the harvest. The last, and most significant, sign is the decree made by the Government that English shall be taught in all the public schools.

The first Japanese Gospel was printed in 1872, and the New Testament in 1880; this year the whole Bible has been issued.

THE INDIAN ARCHIPELAGO

Is far larger and more densely populated than is usually supposed. Borneo, for instance, next to New Guinea and Australia, is the largest island on the earth. Sumatra is 1000 miles long, and as great as Britain. Celebes and Java are each as large as Ireland; whilst the smaller islands, with considerable populations, can be numbered by scores, if not hundreds. Excluding New Guinea and the islands to the eastward, whose inhabitants are of a different race, the population is computed at 34 millions, whose religions are Buddhism and Mohammedanism, modified by aboriginal heathenism.

No English or American Society has missionaries here, and it is best, for national and ecclesiastical reasons, that Christian work should be left to the Dutch in the islands they possess, though it is to be desired that they prosecute it with greater vigour.

The following table indicates the state of the Missions, which are now being carried on by the various Societies, so far as the indifference of the Dutch to give information enables us to impart it :—

[TABLE.

TABLE OF DUTCH MISSIONS IN THE INDIAN ARCHIPELAGO, &c.

Name of Society.	Sphere.	Missionaries.	Native Helpers.	Communicants.
Rhenish Missionary Society,	Dutch East Indies,	31	121	3,450
Netherlands Missionary Society,	{ Celebes, Java, Savoo, Soomba, }	11	47	91,879
Netherlands Missionary Union,	Western Java,	8	13	375
Utrecht Missionary Society,	Almahira,	7	16	61
Java Comité,	Java, Sumatra,	3	15	400
Mennonite Missionary Society,	Java,	3	12	100
Ermelo Missionary Society,	Central Java,	3	...	...
The Christian Reformed Church's Society,	Java,	4	5	60
Dutch Reformed Missionary Society,	Java,	3	12	200
Zeist Auxiliary to the Moravian Society,	{ Surinam (Dutch South America), }	36	162	25,043
Auxiliary to the Rhenish Missionary Society,	......	31	24	832

A number of lay helpers are associated with the Missions. The adherents are not given, and the distinction between nominal and real Christians, which is recognised in English and American Missionary Society reports, is not as apparent in the Dutch ones.

With one exception, all the Societies named in the preceding Table are Dutch. The schools are usually small, and, with the exception of Minnahassa, in Celebes, all the stations are disappointing in their results.

The Rhenish Society seems to be the most energetic of the group. Commencing in Borneo in 1835, it advanced to Sumatra in 1861, and in 1865 to Nias, which, though the smallest of the three, has a population of half-a-million. On the three islands the church members number 8600; thousands are carefully instructed preparatory to baptism, and in various stations the prospects are very bright.

To the east of Celebes runs a chain of some seventy small islands named Sangir, where four of Gossner's missionaries commenced to labour in 1855, who afterward were joined by some Dutch missionaries.

It is singular that none of the Societies named have directed attention to some islands where once the seed of the Gospel was plentifully, if not wisely, sown. Even as early as 1636 one minister had charge of 30,000 converts to the Christian faith. Formerly the islands of Timor, Banda, Ternate, Wittir, Dammor, Tipa, and the rich Moluccas, all had their Christian congregations. In some of them Christianity is altogether extinct; but it is credibly reported that on other islands there still remains an aggregate of 5000 native Christians, without any satisfactory oversight,—sheep without a shepherd.* But it is a startling fact, in contrast with this, that Mohammedanism is at the present time making rapid progress over the whole Indian Archipelago.

---

* "Conference on Foreign Missions," Mildmay, 1878, p. 140.

The Phillipine Islands

Are too much under Portuguese surveillance to be reached by any form of avowed Protestant effort.

New Guinea,

Though so near to Australia, is but little known. It is sufficient here to state that it is larger than France. It is 1490 miles in length, is rich in natural productions, and is inhabited by a great variety of degraded races.

The only Christian agency prior to 1871 was a small unprogressive Mission of the Utrecht Society.

In that year, the London Missionary Society adopted it as a sphere, under circumstances worthy of notice. By its exertions, many islands in the Pacific had not only been Christianised, but so developed in self-reliance and zeal, that they could be left to the care of native ministers, under slight European supervision; and many of the native preachers, having acted with considerable zeal and fidelity as evangelists on islands adjacent to their own, were well trained and were willing to take a part in yet more remote and important enterprises.

The Directors of the Society determined to utilise this valuable and appropriate native agency in connection with the New Guinea Mission; and accordingly two missionaries of tried value, Mr. Macfarlane of Lifu, and Mr. W. G. Lawes, the first missionary of Niue, or Savage Island, were invited to form, with the assistance of volunteer native agents, a series of stations along the New Guinea coast. This has been successfully accomplished in spite of the unknown country, the unhealthy climate, and of barbarism, in some instances breaking out into massacre. Two missionaries from Murray Island, north-east of Queensland, superintend about 72 native evangelists, who at a long line of stations on o near the mainland, pursue their unselfish enterprise; and from Port Moresby, on the south-east coast, other 2 missionaries, assisted by 16 native ministers, and a number of catechists and teachers, spread light from several stations. A third central station at East Cape, at the extreme south-east, has this year been commenced, which opens up a fine, varied, and interesting sphere.

The converts to Christianity number more than 2000; and already New Guinea has its organised churches, its numerous schools, its training colleges, its own native evangelists, and its martyrs. The training college at Murray Island has 60 natives under instruction.

The Rhenish Society has this year commenced to work on the German side of the island; and on the side adjoining Australia an Episcopal Mission is contemplated. Unfortunately, a Jesuit Mission is to work from Yule Island. Its proximity to the stations of the London Society indicate that, with the usual meanness and bigotry of their Church, they will direct their efforts more to harass the Protestants than to convert the Pagans.

New Britain and New Ireland,

East of New Guinea, are the scene of Methodist Missionary effort, under the direction of the Australian Conference. In the former island the Rev. G. Brown commenced a Mission six years ago. The issue for a time was doubtful, but the people now are friendly. Tribal feuds have abated, and some converts have been won.

Australia

Offers no important sphere for Foreign Missions. The aborigines are excessively degraded; they are few, scattered widely apart, and are averse to settled habits. Efforts to reach them have been made, but have been attended with no striking results.

New Zealand,

With an area almost equal to that of England, Scotland, and

Ireland, has a white population of only half-a-million, and a Maori population of only 42,819. The latter receive the attention of no less than seven Societies — the Wesleyan, Church, Propagation, Primitive Methodist, United Methodist, North German, and Hermannsberg Societies. The two former have been most distinctly and extensively missionary, and have won the principal results. Samuel Marsden, in the interests of the Church Missionary Society, laid the foundation of an important Mission in 1814, and Samuel Leigh, in 1818, commenced the Wesleyan Mission.

The results have been that more than 30,000 of the natives have adopted the Christian faith; but that which at one time promised to be a striking triumph of the Gospel, has been marred by error and sin, directly and indirectly introduced by European earth-hunger and immorality.

POLYNESIA.

The Polynesian Missions in their history combine variety, difficulty, romance, and triumph, beyond most others. At the close of last century there was not in the whole of these island groups a single native Christian, or a person who could read or write. Idolatry, with its attendant vice and degradation, was universal, whilst cannibalism, human sacrifices, infanticide, and the murder of the aged and diseased, were common on many islands. How all this has been changed will be seen as we proceed.

The London Missionary Society commenced its splendid work of evangelisation in Tahiti in 1797. In 1812 it began on the Society Islands; in 1816 on the small Austral group; in 1821 on the Harvey Islands; in 1836 on the Samoas; in 1841 on the Loyalty Islands; and about 1861 on the small Ellice, Tokelau, and Gilbert groups.

Tahiti, where the first fruits were gathered, after a long night of weeping, became, in 1836, a scene of solicitude through French interference, with its attendant moral corruption and Roman Catholic intrigues. Happily, the people were so well trained in Scriptural knowledge that they have held fast to the faith first received, so that not a twentieth part of the native population is Romanist. Since 1863 French Protestant Missions have had a recognised influence over the native Christian Churches.

Some of the *Society Islands*, as Raiatea, Borabora, and Huahine, are of considerable size, and from them all heathenism has been swept away. So also in the *Harvey group*.

The *Samoan Islands* have a most interesting missionary history of their own. The Mission was commenced in 1836, and for some time it was violently opposed, but in 1846 nine-tenths of the people had embraced the new faith. Now, of the 35,000 people, 27,000 adhere to the London Missionary Society, whilst the remainder belong to the Wesleyans and Roman Catholics. One of the best institutions for the training of native teachers and ministers in all Polynesia exists on Upolu. Eighty or more are always being trained in it, and since its foundation more than 1800 have been prepared for spheres of usefulness as ministers of Christian Churches, or evangelists to the heathen—in some instances 2000 miles distant.

The *Tokelau, Ellice, and Gilbert groups*, with their 10,136 converts, are under the care of 23 native ministers, who are superintended from Samoa.

The *Loyalty Islands* reveal the usual features of wrong, cruelty, and Romish interference and intrigue, which follow where the French "protect," or seize the territory of a weak and defenceless race. The true work done by Protestants is harassed and hindered, if it cannot be undone, by those whose policy it seems to be to prefer labouring among Protestant converts rather than the heathen.

Besides the groups named, subordinate groups and isolated islands like Niue, with its 5000 inhabitants, have been reached by the agents of the London Society. In several instances every vestige of heathenism has disappeared; in others its adherents are a degraded minority. Altogether the converts number 59,903, the communicants 18,190, the native ministers 259, the native preachers 440, and the European missionaries no more than 24. And these numbers are exclusive of the converts and native agents on *Tahiti* and the *Austral* and *Tuamotu* groups.

The *Sandwich Islands* owe their evangelisation entirely to the American Board, whose missionaries first reached the islands in 1820. By 1848 the eleven islands, with a population at that time estimated at 90,000, had become, in constitution, laws, and religious profession, as decidedly Christian as many of the States of Europe.

As early as 1852, the Christian community there entered definitely on the missionary enterprise, by sending some of their number, along with the American missionaries, to the *Marquesas*, and subsequently to the small and interesting *Marshall* and *Caroline* groups.

The entire cost to the American Board up to the time the people declared themselves a Christian nation, was only £244,000. Seldom has an equal sum of money been as profitably spent. The total number of members admitted into the Churches up to 1870 was 55,300. This gives an expenditure of £4 only for each convert, without taking account of the splendid educational, social, and national results.*

A High Church Mission, with a bishop at Honolulu, was begun—most unnecessarily, as we cannot but think—in 1861. Its five clergy have but a small number of adherents.

The Tongan and Fiji Islands owe their conversion to the Wesleyans. In 1822 they entered on the first-named sphere, and met with rapid and unusual success. There are in the

* "History of the Sandwich Island Mission," by Dr. Rufus Anderson. Hodder & Co., London.

group 126 churches, 8300 communicants, 5000 scholars, and 17,000 who regularly attend public worship, out of a population of 20,000. Political discord has recently disturbed this promising sphere.

The adjacent *Fijis* number about 225, of which 80 are inhabited. The Mission was commenced as recently as 1835. Cannibalism was more common than anywhere else. After a comparatively brief period of severe trial, great numbers of the people felt the power of the Gospel, and now the triumph has become marvellous and complete. Out of a population of 112,000, 102,000 are Methodists, whose religious organisations are thus described:—

Chapels and preaching places,	1,236
Missionaries,	11
Native ministers,	55
Catechists,	40
Teachers,	1,058
Local preachers,	1,785
Communicants,	26,839
Candidates on trial,	4,659
Sunday-school scholars,	42,651

The contributions last year to mission purposes amounted to £4000.

The governor of this now British possession, Sir Arthur Gordon, says:—" It is impossible to speak in too strong terms of the wonderful service and results, both religious and social, which have attended the Wesleyan Missions in Fiji. The condition of the people is as different from what it was as can possibly be conceived. The people of Fiji are now a Christian people."

The New Hebrides consist of 30 islands, inhabited by a wild and treacherous population, estimated to number 100,000. It was in the attempt to place native teachers on Erromanga, one of this group, that John Williams fell, and it is indicative of the heroism born of Missions, that when the news of his death reached Samoa, some of the native teachers immediately volunteered to go to Erromanga. Two landed in 1840, and after some years of alternate hope and disappointment, the Mission passed in 1854, by an amicable arrangement, out of the hands of the London Missionary Society into the care of the Presbyterians of Nova Scotia.

Another of the islands, Anetium, had been similarly transferred six years before. The history of the latter island abounds with romance, dangers, and Christian heroism, and the result is stated in the tablet placed in the church there in memory of Dr. Geddie:—"When he landed in 1848 there were no Christians here; when he left here, in 1872, there were no heathens." But other islands have proved singularly impervious to Christian influences. The mission is now under the charge of a pleasant combination of 16 Presbyterian missionaries from British North America, Australia, New South Wales, New Zealand, Tasmania, and the Free Church of Scotland. The native teachers number 120, the adherents 4000, the communicants 1000, and the scholars 2433.

MICRONESIA,

Includes 4 groups and a number of small, isolated, low-lying, coral islands, extending over an immense expanse of ocean to the north-east of New Guinea.

The four groups of islands classed under this designation are the *Gilbert, Marshall, Caroline,* and *Ladrone Islands,* there being from 50 to 70 in each group.

The first three groups have, from 1852, received most attention from the American Board of Commissioners for Foreign Missions and the native Christians of the Sandwich Islands. Indeed, the latter have found most of the agents and a considerable amount of the funds. The success has been considerable. On the Marshall Islands, with about 10,000 inhabitants, there are 23 church buildings, in which there are 600 church members, representing an adult Christian population at least four times as great.

In the Eastern Carolines there are 728 church members and fifteen places of worship; and in the Central Carolines, 1036 church members and fifteen churches.

In less than forty years there has grown in these islands, from nothing, fifty churches, all self-supporting, with a membership, whose discipline is not lax, of 5000. Yet we are informed that Missions are a failure!

The *Tokelau, Ellice,* and some of the *Gilbert* islands, are cared for by the London Missionary Society. The converts exceed 10,000 and the church members 2300.

From the north-east of New Guinea there extends to Fiji, for a distance of 3500 miles, various island groups, known under the general name of

MELANESIA.

The Papuans, who for the most part inhabit them, are more degraded, violent, and cannibal than the other Polynesian races. Some of the Missions among them have been sketched, but another remains to be noticed.

Bishop Selwyn visited several of these islands in 1848, and to evangelise them adopted the method of bringing, from various islands, youths to be prepared at a common centre to go back to be the Christian teachers of their countrymen. Such a school was opened in New Zealand in 1850, and about forty scholars from various islands were received. In 1860 the school was removed to Mota, in the Banks group; then, in 1866, to Norfolk Island.

But this method of operation has proved to be indirect and tedious, and also very expensive. The results do not appear to be very great. The missionaries, or their native assistants, more or less labour in the Solomon, Santa Cruz, and Banks groups, as well as some isolated islands. They have 2000 scholars in their schools. New Caledonia is within their range, but French policy impedes the attempts of English missionaries.

We have thus sketched the spheres occupied by various Missions in the splendid and numerous islands of the Indian Archipelago and Polynesia.

There are still numerous islands, and some of them of great extent, where no Christian agency is found, as well as others where it is quite inadequate to meet the wants of the people. But it will be seen that some of the most important island groups of the Pacific have been reached by the Gospel, and what has been done is a sure presage of a steady, onward movement to the islands yet heathen.

CHAPTER IX.

MISSION FIELDS AND AGENCIES—AMERICA.

OUTH AMERICA presents but a restricted sphere for Missions to the heathen, yet an abundant, though difficult one to Protestant effort. Various small heathen tribes lead a degraded and precarious existence in most of the Northern and Central States, but their own unsettled habits, and Roman Catholic hostility to all forms of Protestant evangelisation, cause it to be very difficult to reach them with effect.

PATAGONIA AND TIERRA DEL FUEGO,
Situated at the extreme south of the Continent, are heathen, and only partially under Romish despotism; but the region is utterly repellent, and the few wretched and degraded natives seem frozen into apathy toward a faith so pure, elevating, and spiritual as Christianity.

The first attempt to reach the Fuegans was made by Captain Fitzroy in 1830. He induced four natives to accompany him to England; and, after having them instructed, took them back, in company with a zealous Christian named Matthews, who purposed to remain as an evangelist; but the hostility of the people was so marked, and the prospects so gloomy, that he returned in the vessel that took him out.

The next attempt ended in utter disaster; nevertheless, out of it, as the phœnix from the flames, has arisen the only Society which concentrates its energies on South America.

In 1838 Captain Allan Gardiner attempte to settle as a

missionary pioneer among the Auracanian Indians, who hold a somewhat independent position south of the Argentine Republic. Failing in this, after trying other enterprises in South-Eastern Africa, and South America, he succeeded, after great discouragement, in obtaining resources to begin a Mission in Tierra del Fuego. He landed there in 1850 with six coadjutors, but in a few months they all perished miserably, through cold, want, and disease.*

The flag he so bravely, though not wisely, carried was taken up after he fell by others, who developed his plans, and formed the South American Missionary Society. Taking the Falkland Islands as a base, in 1856, it has gradually formed a small Mission among the Fuegans, and three in Patagonia. One of its aims is to reach the heathen tribes scattered farther north, by means of chaplains, who, whilst preaching to Protestant Societies, shall instruct Roman Catholics and Pagan tribes, as occasion serves. Six such stations have been formed, at places like Valparaiso. But in no direction has there been much success.

Dutch and British Guiana,

On the north-east coast, have a very mixed population of Indians, Negroes, and Hindoo and Chinese coolies, amounting to about 400,000. Since 1739 the Moravians, and, from the early years of this century, the Wesleyan, the Propagation, and the London Societies have given a fair amount of attention to the people. About one-half of them are now Christians.

Honduras and Mosquito Coast.

The Methodists and Episcopalians labour in the former territory, and the Moravians in the latter.

The West India Islands

Contain a population of 4,600,000, thus distributed:—

* "The Story of Allan Gardiner," by Rev. J. W. Marsh. "Pioneers and Founders," by Miss Yonge.

In the Spanish possessions, 2,178,000; British, 1,206,000; French, 335,759; Dutch, 42,447; Danish, 33,763; Hayti, 800,000. Spain gives no encouragement to Protestant Missions, and in Hayti the efforts made have not been attended with much success, but in the other possessions much has been accomplished. The first missionaries to the Negroes were two Moravians, who settled on the Island of St. Thomas in 1733. Others settled in Jamaica in 1754; Antigua, in 1756; Barbadoes, in 1765; St. Croix, in 1771; and Tobago in 1790. Nathaniel Gilbert, of Antigua, in 1760, was the first Englishman, apparently, who openly gathered slaves together for public worship; though various instances occur during the century when the friends and agents of the Christian Knowledge and Propagation Societies endeavoured to instruct and evangelise the slaves on the islands and the aborigines on the Continent.

But from 1787 must be dated systematic effort to Christianise the people. In that year Dr. Coke, with three other Wesleyans, commenced services among the Negroes which, with marked results, continue to the present time. The Baptist Society sent its first agents in 1813, and the London Missionary Society in 1834. Since then Episcopalians, Presbyterians, and other Methodists have joined in the work, and with much success. Polytheism has disappeared, and though the Christianity of the Negroes is not of the strongest or noblest type, it yet is very genuine and powerful for good. Some of the various Missions are self-supporting, but efficient Negro pastors are greatly needed.

To the Baptists must be assigned a very distinguished place in the good that has been accomplished throughout the West Indies. Several of their missionaries—as Burchell, Knibb, Phillippo—have been superior men, alike as preachers and men of affairs. They did more to abolish slavery than any other class on the islands. They not only made many converts and formed numerous churches, but have done much to train the people in all manly, self-reliant, and Christian qualities. Their strength in Jamaica may be judged from a membership of 28,900, where the conditions of membership are more strict than usual.

In the small though numerous islands of the Bahamas the Baptists have, in 77 churches, an average attendance of 12,000 worshippers, a membership of 4000, and 5000 Sabbath scholars, all under the direction of one European missionary, with about twenty coloured evangelists. The Wesleyans are also successful. In their six circuits are 3600 church members, 3000 day scholars, and an attendance on public worship of 10,000 persons.

Recently, a new demand for Christian effort has arisen in the West Indies from the extended immigration of coolie labourers from India and China. On Trinidad, for instance, there are about 50,000, among whom the Canadian Presbyterians are labouring; the local Presbytery consisting of four Canadians, one United Presbyterian from Scotland, and a Hindu minister.

The United States

Present some interesting missionary problems. There are, first, the Aboriginal Indians, who now number in the States only 261,851, and of these about 90,000 are Christians. Several Societies attend to their spiritual wants.

But the Negro population demand more strenuous effort. They number 6,500,000, and though nominally Christian, need much instruction and care. This is partially given by the Freedman's Aid and various Home Missionary Societies.

The comparately few—100,000—Chinese settlers are, as far as practicable, brought under Christian instruction.

In Alaska missionary work is still in its infancy. Thither the Moravians sent five of their agents in 1885 to labour amongst the Eskimo. Before 1867, when the territory of Alaska was purchased from Russia by the United States

Government, the only Christian instruction the people had received was what a small Mission conducted by the Greek Church could give. After its acquisition, the American Presbyterians commenced work in the south-east; but as the population was very mixed (Eskimo, Alents, Creoles, Tinneh, Ihlingets, Hydah, and whites), and the Society's resources were already fully taxed, Dr. Sheldon Jackson made several appeals to other Boards, but without effect. At length he turned to the Moravians with the plea, "If you refuse, these heathen must go down in the dark." Such an appeal could not be resisted, and a number volunteered to engage in this unknown service. In the spring of 1885 the first five missionaries went to establish a station, and they now report that they have made progress with the language, have gained the confidence of the people, and are enabled to render medical assistance. Two other volunteers have been sent this year to commence a school at Nushagak.

British North America,

With its 3,600,000 square miles of territory, though almost as large as Europe, is not of great importance as a Foreign Mission field. The total population is less than 5,000,000, and of this comparatively small number, at least 4,500,000 are of European descent. The Indians and Eskimo are not only few in number, but widely scattered in small migratory parties throughout the vast regions of the North-West and on the Pacific Coast. Nevertheless, as persons, their salvation is as important as that of individuals belonging to any race, and great should be the honour paid to those who go into the dreary, inclement regions of the extreme north, to bring home those straying children of the Great Father.

The Church Missionary Society began its successful efforts among them in 1820, and now the Episcopal Missions are thus placed:—

The North-West Mission extends over six immense

though very thinly inhabited dioceses, such as that of Rupert's Land and Moosonee. As much is being accomplished almost as the inclemency of the climate and the depressing condition of the people will permit. Schools are comparatively numerous. Some good native assistants have been obtained, and about 12,000 native Christians have been gathered into churches, of whom about 1600 are communicants.

The North Pacific branch of the same Mission dates only from 1862, and most of its eleven stations have not been formed twelve years. It is under the charge of six clergymen, who are assisted by six native teachers. The converts number almost 1000, and the scholars 450.

In British North America the Moravian Missions are the oldest, though few in number, and not important in results. The Methodists and Roman Catholics are more active and numerous, not without friction with the Missions first named.

LABRADOR

Became, in 1752, the field of labour of one of the first Moravians who went to Greenland, and ever since, with great patience and self-denial, his co-religionists have had a Mission there. If their converts number no more than 1300, the sparseness of the population, and the difficulty of conducting Missions in such an inhospitable region, must be taken in account.

GREENLAND

Has a romantic Christian history. The first authentically known attempt to evangelise it was made by Hans Egede in 1721. His life forms one of the most heroic and pathetic chapters in the history of Missions, and though he saw no conversions, his life has been fruitful of inspiration to the missionary enterprise. He was joined in 1733 by two Moravians, and the work has ever since been sustained by their Church and missionaries from Denmark. The rigid climate, the stolidity of the people, their wandering habits, and their impracticable language have made Mission work unusually trying, and though all but a few score of the people are professing Christians, little is done, or perhaps can be done, to perpetuate Christian truth and ordinances by themselves, or to diffuse them elsewhere, by means of funds and agencies drawn from Greenland.

The following Tables, taken, with variations, from "Warneck's History of Protestant Missions," will fittingly close this review.

They do not precisely agree with the figures given elsewhere; but the substantial harmony thus exhibited is clear evidence of all the accuracy that can be required, and is more than might have been expected. It is in itself a suggestive fact that accuracy is almost an exclusively Christian quality, and that whilst very few Pagan races ever attempt to take a census of the people, none are reliable, as those of Christian nations are. The numbers given, therefore, relative to Asiatic and African races are estimates only, but since they are formed usually on a broad and varied basis of facts, and by men of tried knowledge, judgment, and impartiality, they may be accepted as the nearest approximation to truth that under the circumstances is practicable.

According to Behm and Wagner,—Supplement 69 to Petermann's "Geographical Information,"—the population of the world is as follows:—

Europe,	327,743,400
Asia,	795,591,000
Africa,	205,823,260
America,	100,415,400
Australia and Polynesia,	4,232,000
Polar Regions,	82,509
Total,	1,433,887,560

TABLE OF ADHERENTS ASSOCIATED WITH PROTESTANT MISSIONS.

I. America.

1. Greenland and Labrador,	10,300
2. North American Indians,	130,000
3. West Indies,	407,800
4. Central and South America,	130,000
	678,100

II. South Seas.

1. Polynesia,	380,000
2. Micronesia,	16,000
3. Melanesia,	16,000
4. New Zealand,	40,000
5. Australia,	1,000
	453,000

III. Asia.

1. Indian Archipelago,	150,000
2. India,	450,000
3. Ceylon,	38,000
4. Burmah,	80,000
5. China,	60,000
6. Japan,	10,000
7. Other Countries of Asia,	35,000
	823,000

IV. Africa.

1. North Africa,	1,000
2. West Africa,	120,000
3. South Africa,	250,000
4. East Africa,	1,000
5. African Islands,	300,000
	672,000

Total.	2,626,100

TABLE OF THE RELIGIONS OF THE WORLD.

RELIGIONS.	Europe.	Asia.	Africa.	America.	Australia and Polynesia.	TOTAL.
Jews,	5,137,000	800,000	938,000	137,000	10,000	7,022,000
Mohammedans,	5,974,600	128,000,000	53,000,000	......	......	185,974,000
Hindus,	......	190,000,000	100,000	86,000	......	190,186,000
Buddhists, Shintoists, Taoists, Confucians,	......	400,000,000	200,000	156,000	40,000	400,396,000
Undefined and Sects,	211,000	8,304,000	......	106,000	295,000	3,916,000
Heathen,	258,000	78,000,000	158,000,000	9,244,000	4,373,000	249,895,000
Total non-Christians,	11,580,000	805,104,000	212,238,000	9,729,000	4,738,000	1,042,389,000
Romanists,	110,000,000	1,429,000	699,000	37,540,000	454,000	180,315,000
Protestants,	81,500,000	1,830,000	940,000	39,380,000	2,500,000	129,150,000
Greek Church,	71,000,000	5,000,000	......	......	......	76,000,000
Armenians, Kopts, Abyssinians,	1,000,000	4,800,000	4,800,000	......	......	10,600,000
Undefined Confessions,	100,000	1,013,000	501,000	815,000	22,600	2,461,600
Total Christians,	296,600,000	14,072,000	6,940,000	77,735,000	2,976,600	397,526,600
Total all Religions,	308,180,000	819,176,000	219,178,000	87,464,600	7,714,000	1,439,915,600

CHAPTER X.

THE RESULTS OF MISSIONS.

N inquiry into the results of Missions is alike important and interesting. Thousands of men and women, for the most part well trained and educated, have, during the past ninety years, been sent and sustained at an aggregate cost of £20 million sterling, into every part of the Pagan world, for the express purpose of persuading the people to abandon their ancestral religions, and receive instead the sublime, though self-denying, Christian faith. Has any reasonable amount of success attended this enterprise? The answer to this question greatly concerns all who are interested in the progress and elevation of our race, whether they be friendly, or indifferent, or hostile to the Missionary idea. We have no hesitation in giving an affirmative reply to the inquiry, and shall support our assertion by an abundant array of facts. But before adducing this evidence, and that its due weight may be understood, it is important to state clearly and distinctly the conditions of the missionary problem.

I. In attempting to form a just estimate of the results of Foreign Missions, *five conditions* of the enterprise must be taken into account:—

1. Missionaries generally are sent to unhealthy and uncongenial regions. They are foreigners, unused to the climate, ignorant of its requirements, unfamiliar with the customs of the people, having no knowledge of their character, and

little of their modes of thought. They live and labour, for the most part, among ignorant or semi-civilised races, who are intensely suspicious and distrustful; and they have to begin at the beginning. They have to learn a language entirely different to their own, and, if possible, to learn it so well that they can speak it with accuracy and effect. In most cases the language has to be reduced to an alphabetical form; in all, the Scriptures and Christian books have to be translated into it. Christians have to be made out of heathen; schools have to be formed, and teachers trained; and Christian societies have to be organised, trained, and developed.

2. Under any circumstances, even the most favourable, the enterprise of changing the religion of a race, or even of a tribe, is a most formidable undertaking.

All history shows how reluctant nations are to change their religion, how seldom they do change, and with what convulsive effort the change is effected. This has been so, whether the gods worshipped were such as Woden, Thor, and Balder, or Jupiter, Mars, and Venus; whether they were mere African or Polynesian fetishes, feared by petty tribes, or divinities such as Allah, Buddha, Brumha, Vishnu, or Seva, whose worship has spread through empires, become venerable by the associations of a thousand years, and strong by being inwoven with the hopes and fears, the customs, habits, and idiosyncrasies of tens of millions of worshippers.

Changes and modifications, even in a religion, are slowly and almost imperceptibly introduced—as when Vedic Hinduism grew into Puranism, and Apostolic Christianity into Popery. But the definite repudiation of one religion in favour of another is of rare occurrence. Three religions only, according to Max Müller, are missionary in essence, and have wrought such revolutions—Buddhism, Islam, and Christianity. But Buddhism absorbed and assimilated, rather than destroyed, the excessively weak and undogmatic superstitions it found in Burmah, China, and Japan; and it has made little progress for a thousand years. Mohammedanism owed its triumphs in Western Asia and Northern Africa more to the race and religious degeneracy of the countries it overran, than to the vigour and fanaticism which inspired the Arabs and their auxiliaries, great as these were. Nevertheless, though favoured by a singular combination of circumstances, it required heroic effort, through some generations, to secure its triumph.

Christianity has triumphed over enormous difficulties and by legitimate agencies, as no other faith has ever done. But how stupendous were the tasks of converting the diverse races of the Roman empire, and the barbarians of Western and Northern Europe! What faith, patience, love, heroism, and self-denial were expended by myriads of Christian souls along weary generations ere the victories were won!

Nevertheless, in spite of history, and in contempt of probability, the friends of Missions too often expect barbarous tribes, and Asiatic kingdoms and empires, which have changed in nothing, purposely, for a thousand years, and hate and dread new ideas, to be converted almost with the rapidity with which Cæsar came, and saw, and conquered his Gallic enemies! It is demonstrable that the evangelisation of Africa is a more stupendous undertaking than was the conversion of all the tribes of Central and Northern Europe; and that of India alone than of the Roman Empire. According to Gibbon, the Roman Empire, when at its greatest, had a population of 150,000,000, whilst India has 253,000,000. And this is but one of many features of comparison. The former was converted by men of the same colour and of similar race, and they had not to face a strange and most unhealthy climate, or any obstacle half so formidable as caste.

3. The reluctance of any considerable number of human beings, in any country, to receive a religion, pure, strict, and self-denying as Christianity must be taken into account.

It is more difficult to persuade persons to embrace this religion than any other, because it makes demands on everyone to whom it is offered which seem to the great mass of mankind severe, humiliating, and hard. Every one, even in a country like our own, who endeavours to lead others to follow the true Christian life, is made painfully conscious of this. And the difficulty is intensified among the heathen, because the state of mind and life induced by almost all forms of false religions is as opposed to the New Testament ideal of life and character as it well can be. It is not, for instance, half as difficult (in some instances, it is not difficult at all), for an African fetish-worshipper to become a Mohammedan; or a Chinese Taoist a Buddhist; or a Polynesian idolator to discard one god for another; as it is to persuade any of them to become a Christian. The former is little more than a change of name. The latter means a change of heart and life, moral and social revolution and innovation. What missionary in Eastern lands has not heard from those, who, if not steeped to the lips in vice, were yet left at liberty by their surroundings to sin almost as much as they pleased, such expressions as—" Your religion is too good." " No one can be as good and virtuous as you urge us to be."

It is to the honour of Protestant missionaries, almost without exception, that whilst seeking to propagate a faith which bears much the same relation to the superstitions of Asia and Africa, as virtue does to vice and light to darkness, they have prosecuted their enterprise with an openness as to their aims, a courage in the condemnation of all sin and error, a candour as to the demands made on their converts to be true, holy, and good, and peaceable and respectful toward authority, such as has characterised no other propagandists, be they political, social, or religious. Christianity makes heavier demands on the self-denial of its disciples than any other religion; and if it be only profound conviction, or deep, true feeling, or great courage, that will move most

Englishmen to profess godliness, it must require a greater amount of these, than is usually supposed, to lead a devil-worshipper in Tinnevelly, a Vishnuvite in Bengal, or the devotee of some hideous idol in Polynesia to renounce their worship, and to attempt to be pure and good and true. Nor are the adherents of faiths more advanced—like Buddhism, Mohammedanism, and Bramhoism—easier to win; for the social and intellectually subtle fetters which hold them are fascinating and strong to a degree few can understand, who are unfamiliar with the immobility, servility, and moral laxity of Eastern races.

All this should be taken into account when the results of Missions are judged; but it is illustrative of the irrational prejudice with which they are regarded, that missionaries are considered visionaries and fanatics for even attempting to convert the heathen, and are reproached and ridiculed for failure if they do not succeed, or with credulity and something worse if they speak of success.

4. The proportion of missionaries sent to those they have to evangelise must also be considered.

It is an accepted principle, admitting of very varied application, that a cause must be adequate to the production of a given result. An invading army, for instance, ought, in number and equipment, to be sufficiently strong to meet and triumph over all probable opposition. But it will be seen that the Christian army sent out to evangelise the heathen world bears no adequate proportion to the vast populations it has to influence.

We have seen that the population of our earth, outside all forms of Christianity, numbers 1035 millions, and the missionaries sent among them by all Protestant Churches number, at the highest computation, not more than 6000, or one to each 174,166 of the heathen world. That is, about three to populations equal to those of Manchester, Liverpool, and Birmingham; two to those of Sheffield and Leeds; one to those of Hull and Newcastle; two to the counties of Cornwall, Leicestershire, and Suffolk; and one to Bedfordshire, Bucks, and Oxfordshire.*

There are 120,000 ministers of religion for the Protestants of Europe and America, or one for each 960 of the people. If this proportion be compared with that of missionaries to the heathen, whether we call the former 6000 or 4500, it will be manifest that the phrase, too often heard, "we have heathens enough at home, we must care for them," is acted on with a selfishness which calls itself wise, but which no one can prove to be Christian.

If such contrasts are analysed, they exhibit the disproportion of agency in a yet more striking light. There are, for instance, in Bath and Bristol, with a population of 400,000, about as many ministers of religion as in all China, with its 300,000,000 of people. So Manchester, each Riding of Yorkshire, even Devonshire, with its 603,000 of population, severally have the services of about as many ministers of religion as India, with its 253 million people, more open to every form of Christian effort than the people of any other non-Christian land.

If, further, the comparison be extended to subsidiary agencies, the contrast will be seen to be yet more striking. There are 30,000 native agents, variously termed ministers, preachers, catechists; but against these are to be placed the

* We have presented the most favourable aspect of the question; but it is not the most accurate. The utmost numerical strength of the Foreign Missionary force is: Ordained missionaries, 2908; lay missionaries, 699; lady missionaries, 2322—or a total of 5929. But a considerable number of the lay missionaries are only partially engaged in real missionary work; and this is so of a large proportion of the lady missionaries. More than half the number given are the wives of missionaries, and, however missionary in sentiment, should hardly be numbered with the avowed and practical workers. Then, further, about 10 per cent. of the missionaries are usually on furlough, so that it is more accurate to estimate the missionary strength at 4500, rather than at 6000.

great army of town missionaries, evangelists, and lay preachers, the Sunday-school teachers, so numerous in England and America, and happily not unknown elsewhere, and finally, the far-extending sweet and holy influences which are exerted by a countless number of devout persons throughout Christian society, to which, alas! there is nothing to compare in most Pagan lands.

5. The Christian agencies now at work abroad, few and inadequate as they are, have a very recent origin. Nine-tenths of them have come into existence within the last seventy years, and much during the last thirty. These periods, though considerable in human lives, are short in the intellectual and moral growth of tribes, races, and empires. Two hundred and fifty years of apostolic and post-apostolic zeal passed before the Roman Empire became, in a most defective sense, Christian. A yet longer period elapsed before Germany and Scandinavia were won from heathenism. It is 1300 years at least since Christianity was first preached in England; yet how far are we even now, with all our splendid religious organisations, from the true ideal of a Christian nation, and how slowly and through what struggles have we risen even to where we are. All evil ways die hard in a world like ours, and all things great and good grow slowly, and with much effort. If in England, with all our knowledge, civilisation, and educated conscientiousness, old customs, vested interests, and evil ways, are so slowly, and with so much difficulty overthrown, it might be expected that barbarous superstitions and customs, such as those prevalent throughout Africa and Polynesia, and great religious systems like those dominant throughout the East, which for a thousand, and even two thousand years have fascinated the imaginations and flattered the idiosyncrasies of vast and powerful races, would with yet greater difficulty, and much more slowly, be overcome.

These observations are not in the least made as if an

apology for the results of Missions were required. None is required; none will be given. On the contrary, we challenge the closest investigation into these results, assured that success, not failure, is their great leading feature.

II. An immense amount of *preparatory pioneer work* has been done.

Since Missions are placed in countries varying in climate from the cold of Greenland to the heat of Scinde, and among races diverse in many respects as Fuegans, Negroes, Polynesians, Syrians, Hindus, and Tartars, a great variety of obstacles have had to be overcome before missionaries could prosecute their direct work, in seeking the conversion of the people.

In some countries, for instance, permission to labour has only been granted after years of weary waiting—as in China, Japan, and many South Sea Islands.

In others, the permission to labour has been purchased from barbarous, despotic, and greedy rulers, like those of Eastern and Central Africa, at a doubtful expenditure of presents and humiliation, and even then the permission has been liable at any moment to be withdrawn.

In many instances, as in Madagascar, India, New Guinea, and Central Africa, missionaries have died or had to abandon their work, through want of knowledge of the conditions of the climate, and of the suitable seasons when its dangers were the least.

Most of the regions where Missionaries are active are unfavourable to the health of Europeans.

In some countries distrust and dislike of foreigners, as in China and Thibet; in others religious fanaticism, as in all Mohammedan States; in others, misconceptions of our designs, as in Uganda and Zululand; in others, caste and race prejudices, as throughout India; have made Missions very difficult, and in many instances impracticable.

Apart from race and religious prejudices, almost all Pagan

are excessively suspicious and distrustful, and utterly sceptical respecting the disinterested and benevolent motives of missionaries; it has, therefore, usually been difficult to gain permission to live among them, and yet more so to win their confidence.

In every country where missionaries labour, they have had to begin at the beginning. They have had to gain possession of the ground, to clear it, to lay the foundations, as well as build the superstructure. They have had to learn languages, to reduce them to written forms; to translate the Bible and Christian books, to prepare all school apparatus. They have had to disarm opposition, to win confidence, and ascertain how most effectively to present Christian truth and duty to minds usually alien to both. They have had to gather scholars out of barbarous, ignorant, idle families, to make Christians out of heathen, and train weak, dissolute, childish natures toward spiritual purity and strength, in spite of inveterate habits, and surrounding vice and crime. They have had not only to establish, strengthen and settle them in the new faith, but to make out of them schoolmasters, evangelists, and ministers.

All this has been done in hundreds, and much of it in thousands, of instances; for it is a significant fact, that in more than 2100 principal, and a far greater number of subordinate stations, converts have been made, Christian societies have been organised, and active propagandist methods adopted.

The entire Bible has been translated into every one of the great languages which are spoken throughout the Pagan world, and the New Testament has been translated into many others. The importance of this, and the labour and scholarship which it has required, are so immense that they cannot easily be described.

In many countries a considerable number of Christian books exist, and much evangelistic literature, from tracts to scholarly treatises on the evidences of Christianity, have been prepared and put in circulation.

Many printing presses belong to the various Missions. Some of them issue annually millions of pages of pure and useful literature. Some are self-supporting, others largely so.

All this is speedily written, and more lightly read; but will the reader try to consider what it includes! Or turn, for its ample illustration and evidence, to the lives of Egede in Greenland, Morrison in China, Judson in Burmah, Gardiner in South America, Moffat in South Africa, Williams in Polynesia, Ziegenbalg in Southern India, and Carey and Thomas in Bengal.

III. Notwithstanding all difficulties, the *direct results* of Missions have been great.

Some of them have already been given in another form, but that they may be the more distinctly seen, we give the more important of them in the following Table :—

Country.	Adherents.	Communicants.	Native Ordained Missionaries.	Evangelists.
South Africa,	250,000			
Burmah,	79,000	25,500	140	400
Ceylon,	37,708	7,500	106	150
Celebes,	40,000			
China,	60,000			
West Indies,	407,300			
India,	450,000	140,000	490	2288
Madagascar,	300,000			
Sandwich Islands,	80,000			
The Fijis,	102,000			
Samoan Islands,	31,000			

To these must be added numerous though smaller groups of converts in other regions; the whole giving a total of about 2,600,000 converts to Christianity, of whom 769,201 are communicants.

Certain considerations will add to the significance of these numbers.

1. To them must be added the tens of thousands who have died in the faith. And whilst instances of calm peace and even triumph in death, are so numerous that the manner in which Christians die has come to be a subject of wonder in some Pagan lands, there is, we believe, no instance on record of one at the end repenting that he had changed his faith.

2. This number of converts is small in comparison with the more than thousand millions of the Pagan world. Nevertheless, it exceeds the population of Wales; it is more than half that of Scotland; it is greater than that of Ulster; it equals that of the West Riding of Yorkshire; it exceeds that of Liverpool, Manchester, Birmingham, and Glasgow combined; and it is not far short of that of all Australia.

3. This Christian population is increasing at a rapid rate; and the increase advances each decade at an accelerated ratio. This might be shown by a numerous array of facts. but two or three will suffice.

The *Missionary Review* of Princeton, America, in the number for November-December, 1885, gives, as the result of one year's labours, an increase of $15\frac{1}{2}$ per cent. on the communicants of all Protestant Missions. It is fair to assume that the same rate of increase prevails among converts and native agents.

Again, the native Christian population of India was in

1851,	91,092
1861,	138,731
1871,	224,258
1881,	417,372

Thus the rate of increase during the first decade was 53 per cent., in the second 61, and in the third 86, whilst the proportionate increase in communicants, native ordained ministers, and evangelists was yet greater.

Again, sixty years ago, there were not ten Protestant Chinese converts; but according to Mr. Donald Mathieson, there were in

1853,	350
1863,	2000
1873,	8000
1883,	22,000

Some place the recent numbers much higher. In 1878 Dr. Legge estimated them at 50,000, and said:—"The converts have multiplied during thirty-five years at least two thousand-fold—the rate of increase being greater year by year." * In Japan the rate of increase is yet greater, being estimated at 500 added to the Christian communities monthly.

4. Certain characteristics of this varied and considerable Christian population are worthy of notice.

(*a*) It falls short of the moral and spiritual standard recognised in avowedly religious society in England, though the Christian members and communicants approach it; but it rises far above the level of general society here.

(*b*) The converts have become distinctly separate from the heathenish beliefs and practices of their neighbours—far more so than in the early and medieval ages of the Church.

(*c*) They are growing in intelligence, manners, comfort, wealth, and influence, as none of the people or the classes around them are.

(*d*) Along with growing numbers and social progress, have come consolidation, energy, and strength. Their ranks are being recruited from the middle and upper classes of society. They are not despised as they were. Their self-reliance is advancing. Being more intelligent and better educated than

* "Conference on Foreign Missions," Mildmay, 1878.

those around them, they know they are on the side of reason, of truth, and of goodness. They know, too, that they are on the winning side. It tells powerfully in their favour in many ways, that the faith they have espoused is that of all really strong, civilised, and advancing races.

(e) They are growing in independence and missionary zeal. The native preachers are not only far more numerous than formerly—they are better trained, and maturer Christians. Still more significant is it, that the number of ordained native ministers has increased more than twenty-fold during the last thirty years. Usually they are carefully selected and trained, and have been too slowly, rather than hastily, entrusted with ministerial responsibilities; and their number is one of the truest signs of the growing strength and stability of the churches in heathen lands. But the advance is all along the line, and not merely among the officers. The number who are impelled to voluntary, independent work by their own love and zeal is increasing, though by no means as great as it should be. So is the amount of money contributed to various Missionary Societies, and to benevolent objects generally. So is the number of self-supporting, self-governing native Christian societies; and so is the number which relies less and less on external government and support.

Many illustrations of this advance might be given. At the recent jubilee of Bishop Sargent, the contrast between the work of the Church Missionary Society in Tinnevelly, then and when he entered India, was thus stated:—

		1835.	1885.
Native Christian Adherents,	. .	8,693	56,286
Communicants,	. . .	114	11,246
Native Ordained Ministers,	. .	1	68
Christian Teachers,	. . .	183	700
Boys at School,	. . .	2,257	10,693
Girls at School,	. . .	147	2,573
Contributions, ... Rs.		0	33,075

The great Mission of the London Society in Madagascar is, in several directions, an evidence of this advance. It has 28 stations and 1133 out-stations under its care, which require, of course, not only the conduct of Sabbath services, but a large amount of pastoral care. The 27 European missionaries are, of course, quite unable to compass either; but they have the large number of 828 native ministers and 4395 preachers to assist them.

Missionary work in some fields is largely in the hands of native auxiliaries, and, in a great number, far more so than formerly. Thus, the New Guinea Mission, which has never had in its brief fifteen years history more than 5 European missionaries at its stations, has 34 natives who rank as ministers, and a considerable staff of evangelists.

In many islands in the South Seas this process has developed from the evangelistic into the pastoral. Islands where there are Christians who have grown strong, are left under the care of native pastors, with visitation from the missionaries, more or less general. The complaint has often been made, and for reasons more than sufficient, that native assistants cling too tenaciously to positions of dependence; but self-reliance, faith in God, and other noble impulses, are evoking, here and there, instances of true missionary zeal. One such only can now be mentioned. Babu Mothura Nath Bose was a student in the Free Church College, Calcutta, where he attained to full university honours. He subsequently became a Brahmic disciple of Kesub Chunder Sen, and, in 1865, was received into the Free Church. Though in business, he began to preach, but, as he came into clearer light, and obtained more joy and peace in believing, a great desire possessed him to be wholly set free for Christ's service. There were, as generally there are when any true, great, and noble work is contemplated, obstacles in the way. He had that shrinking from an independent and responsible course which characterises his race. He inherited its love of money and its pride of position, and both were gratified by an ample income. But the nobler and more Christian motives triumphed, and, abandoning his secular position, he resolved, trusting in God, to consecrate his time and energies to direct Christian work. Thus he is occupied in a large district in Bengal, where the labourers are few; and that he is mainly supported by a native friend and fellow-Christian, is not the least gratifying feature of the case.

Other incidents, not, perhaps, as striking, but pointing in the same direction, are very numerous. Here are a few, rapidly grouped and succinctly stated:—Numbers of the best trained native ministers in India, receive smaller salaries than they could obtain in other positions. There are at least a few marked instances of similar self-sacrifice on the part of Burmese and Chinese evangelists. The money test cannot be applied in the same manner to Malagasi and Polynesians; but both, in numerous instances, have sacrificed comforts, endured hardships, and faced perils, which, in their heathen state, they never voluntarily would have done for any moral or religious cause; and these have been endured for Christ's sake, not only by native preachers of various ranks, but by thousands, and even tens of thousands, of professing Christians. Yes, even unto death they have been faithful. The noble army of martyrs has received many into its ranks even in this age; for let us not only think, and that, too, proudly, as well as sorrowfully, of men of our own race like Bishop Hannington, but of the numerous confessors of Madagascar and Uganda who have dared to meet death in some of its most dreadful forms. There is much in too many native Christians that is weak and defective; but there is much in multitudes of them that is manly, saintly, and even heroic; and it is no boast, but the simple truth, to affirm, that there are numerous converts in every great Mission field who would not hesitate for a moment, if the dread alternative were placed before them, of apostacy or a dreadful death.

There is another feature of native Christian character relating to our present subject worthy of more observation. Heathenism causes its votaries to be poor, selfish, indifferent to the welfare of others, and averse to combine for good objects. Christianity tends to correct all this. Practically, it does not do so among ourselves to as great an extent as one might expect or desire; neither does it among converts from heathenism. But it is operative. And the signs are numerous that it is growingly so. Much already stated is evidence of this. But take such facts as the following, which might be indefinitely multiplied. The 5070 inhabitants of Niue, or Savage Island, contributed in the year 1886-7 the sum of £495, 10s. 2d. to the funds of the London Missionary Society. The Society Islands contribute £821, 13s. 3d. The Methodist converts on some islands display similar liberality. "The leading Wesleyan circuits in Northern Ceylon are not only self-supporting, but are establishing Missions of their own to evangelise the outlying regions." The Baptist converts in Burmah are pursuing the latter course. The Bassein branch of the American Baptist Mission, in the same country, has from its commencement, almost fifty years ago, pursued the policy of self-support, and with admirable results; and, finally, at the foreign stations occupied by the London Missionary Society, there was raised in the year 1886-7 £19,343, one-sixth of its entire income, and a sum equal to its highest annual income prior to 1818. These facts surely go to prove that Missions are successful and reproductive, not only in the higher spiritual sense, but even on the lower principles by which the world judges.

One of the results of Missions, by no means made as prominent as occasionally it should be, is the number of Christian communities nurtured into life by Missions, and then left to themselves or other agencies. This process, if in some instances too long delayed, is in others too hastily adopted, with the result that immature communities are left to contend with difficulties too great for their strength; and thus the gratitude which otherwise they would have to their parent Society, and would cause them to be its glory and support, is dried up. However hard and unwise some Mission Boards have been in the latter direction, there are in the West Indies, South Africa, Madagascar, Polynesia, India, Burmah and other places, numerous communities which owe their existence to Missions, which more or less witness for Christ in dark places, though usually unnoticed in reports.

IV. The *indirect results* of Missions are not only far greater than is usually supposed, they are also even much more important. This must be shown.

The great aim of the missionary is to lead all he can sufficiently influence, to become Christians of the New Testament type, by faith in Christ and obedience to His teaching and example. In attempting to gain this great end, and having in view the ignorance, vice, and degradation usually associated with false religion, he will not only preach the Gospel in the sense in which that term is used among ourselves, but in the manner in which it was preached by Paul throughout the heathen provinces of the Roman empire. The missionary finds it necessary to declare all spiritual truth relating to God, His law, and His claims, to expose the falseness of heathenism, and to protest against its errors and crimes. His manner of life also represents civilisation, purity, goodness and beneficence; features probably altogether new to those among whom he lives.

Attention to him and his aims is probably stimulated by some knowledge of the strange, powerful races, with their impressive ways, from whom the missionary comes. As travellers, trading merchants, settlers, rulers, men belonging to Christian races, are found everywhere, and although too frequently their conduct and the teaching of the missionaries have little in common, they represent that which exerts enormous influence over all native races, and especially uncivilised ones,—power, wealth, and novelty. They bring with them also, though in forms far from perfect, new ideas of God, of justice, of right, and of humanity. During the past two centuries, and especially the nineteenth, the civilised world—which means the Christian world—has been in various ways, pressing itself on the attention of the uncivilised world—which means the non-Christian also. Thus, to a remarkable extent, inquiry has been elicited respecting the religious beliefs which underlie all this greatness, power, and civilisation. And this has led multitudes everywhere to listen attentively and respectfully to those who are the avowed and best qualified teachers of the great Christian faith, and to send their children to the schools everywhere established by the missionaries.

As the result of these forces acting so variously, yet so powerfully, on the inert masses all over Asia and Africa, we see not only hundreds of thousands of converts, who have had sufficient courage and grace to break away from their ancestral superstitions, and to embrace Christian truth, but yet greater numbers who more or less have received some of its teaching, so that their religious opinions and their ideas of the sentiments and customs of their countrymen, differ considerably from those of their fathers.

For instance, throughout the West Indies, Africa, Madagascar, Polynesia, India, China, and Japan, an intellectual, social, and religious change is taking place similar to that which passes over nature when winter begins to be moved and melted by the benign influences of the spring. That which the late Kesub Chunder Sen and Sir Bartle Frere described a few years ago as a quiet yet powerful revolution passing over India, is more or less true of all the regions we have named, and even of some others.

Slavery, with its nameless horrors, has in some countries been abolished; in others its evils have been curtailed; and in others it is threatened as it never yet has been.

This is equally true of evils as repulsive, though not as widespread—infanticide, cannibalism, and human sacrifices.

The wrongs and disabilities affecting womankind are being challenged and rectified as they never have been before.

The manners and customs of many races are softening and improving.

Knowledge is spreading. The great truths and facts of the Bible are more widely known, and by a far greater number of persons all over the heathen world than in any previous age.

The Christian idea, for instance, of God as a Being infinitely perfect, and beneficent, is taking the place not only of the gross polytheisms of Africa and the islands of the sea, but of the vague unsatisfying monotheisms of the great religions of Asia.

So the Christian idea of the soul and of a future life is displacing the gross ideas of heathenism, and the subtle errors of Hindu and Buddhist transmigration.

So the Christian conception of morals, virtue, and goodness as principles of life, are gaining at least the intellectual respect and admiration of multitudes in many lands beyond the limits of Christianity.

So, too, are the Christian ideas, as interpreted by Protestants, of the blessings of knowledge, liberty of conscience, right and justice, truth and honour, the respect due to all men, and the duty of seeking the good of all.

There is an awakening of thought and activity, especially in relation to religion, over most of the immense Pagan world, such as has never taken place in any previous age. Christian missionaries are the prime agents in producing all this; and as it originates with Christianity, so it is a distinct movement towards Christianity, though in very various degrees of development. The spring comes slowly. Long before its sweet though potent influence is seen, it is felt.

In all its operations there is an invisible influence before there is a visible effect. And whilst all growth is gradual and usually slow, it has its degrees; for all forms of vegetation march to maturity not in the mass, but in rank and file. The crocus and the snow-drop appear before the hedges are seen to bud, and these begin to open before the fruit trees blossom. So a similar process of growth towards Christianity is perceptible in many lands, of which the thousands or tens of thousands of avowed converts in each are but the vanguard. It would be alike easy and interesting to exhibit the various signs of this movement in Madagascar, India, Japan, and elsewhere; but let us rather select spheres of Christian evangelisation where the various stages of this march upward and onward are quite discernible.

There are many islands in the Pacific which were entirely heathen at the birth of multitudes yet living, which now are Christian. In Rarotonga, Huahine, Raiatea, Niue, and many other islands, and in some groups—as the Fiji, Tongan, and Sandwich islands—all the outward signs of heathenism—idols, temples, and idolatrous worship—have quite disappeared; and in their place are seen all the signs of Christian influence—churches, schools, a well-kept Sabbath, and a corresponding change in the morals and manners of the people.

In other instances—through the Samoan, Loyalty, Micronesian, and Melanesian groups—the same result is being approached.

Turning elsewhere, the West Indies are a new province added to Christianity in our times.

If the population of Madagascar is not yet Christian, the Government is. In less than half a century it has passed not only in profession, but in principle and policy, from heathenism and barbarism to Christianity and civilisation, and these, too, of a more consistent and emphatic type than characterises most European Governments.

Missionaries may claim no small share in the honour, not only of arousing the Japanese from the sleep of ages, but in guiding them on their remarkable career of progress.

But India offers the best and most varied evidence, and that, too, on the largest scale, of the indirect, as well as the direct effects of Christian example and teaching. Numerous proofs of this could be given. For instance—

It is the opinion of many, who are most familiar with the thoughts and feelings of the people, that there are as many secret as open converts.

It is yet more certain that there are hundreds of thousands, especially in the higher and more respectable classes of society, who, chiefly in consequence of a fair, and in not a few instances, a superior education, have lost faith in idols and have become Monotheists; and if their Monotheism is defective, it at least approaches far nearer to that of the Bible than to that of the Vedas, or the schools of philosophy.

So the gross repulsiveness of transmigration, which constitutes the chief strength of caste, is melting into the Christian conception of the soul, and its responsibility to God for moral conduct.

So public sentiment on such essential questions as caste and the true position of women is greatly altered.

Nor is it opinion only that has changed. Even among a people intensely conservative, who dread and dislike change, such changes are powerfully at work.

The first great social change was the abolition of suttee; and the importance of that event few can imagine.*

Infanticide, which for many generations annually destroyed

---

* In Bengal, from 500 to 700 widows annually thus perished. And many of them were mere children. Between 1815 and 1820, there came under the notice of Government, 62 instances of girls under 18 years of age thus dying. Of these, ten were only of the age of 12; one was 10, and 3 were only 8.

hundreds of thousands of children, is now prohibited throughout British India. If we had done nothing more than stop these two frightful usages, England would have well earned the gratitude of the civilised world.

And usages, if not as cruel and amenable to law, yet quite as pernicious in their influence, are now more or less condemned by public opinion. For instance,

Child marriages, hitherto customary everywhere and among all classes, are felt to be fraught with evil.

Perpetual widowhood, with all the wrongs and sorrows which it has inflicted year by year, for generations, on more than 20 million women, is now acknowledged to be unjust and pernicious.

Female education, which formerly was quite exceptional, and as a policy greatly condemned, is rapidly becoming common.

Kulin polygamy is now held to be disreputable and demoralising.

Caste prejudices are giving way.

Idolatrous rites and ceremonies are neither as immoral, as expensive, nor as popular as they were.

Ample evidence of change in these and many other directions affecting religion could easily be given. The following is quite sufficient, and is derived from very various sources :—

"Everything in India is in a state of revolution," wrote the late Sir Bartle Frere. "Happily for mankind, it is as yet peaceable; generally silent, and often almost unnoticed; but still it is a revolution—more general, more complete, and more rapid than that which is going on in Europe."*

The Rev. B. W. Badley, an American missionary, says :— "Many often tell us in the villages and bazaars, 'Sir, we shall not accept Christianity, we are too old to change, but our children will certainly become Christians.'"

* "Indian Missions," p. 3.

A respectable man said to a member of the civil service in the Punjaub: "Tell your missionaries not to despair. There is something taking place they know nothing about. The whole ground is undermined, and sooner than they expect all will become Christians."

Years ago the late Kesub Chunder Sen said: "The spirit of Christianity has already pervaded the whole atmosphere of Indian Society, and we breathe, think, feel, move in a Christian atmosphere. Native society is being roused, enlightened and reformed under the influence of Christianity." On a subsequent occasion he said: "Our hearts are touched, conquered, overpowered by a Higher Power; and this power is Christ. Christ, not the British Government, rules India! No one but Christ has deserved the precious diadem of the Indian crown, and He will have it."

"From what I know of the Hindoos," said Max Müller to the late Dr. Norman M'Leod, "they seem to me riper for Christianity than any other nation that ever accepted the Gospel."

Similar testimony, from Indian officials of wide experience, could be multiplied,[*] but only one of the most recent will be given.

Sir Rivers Thompson, late Lieutenant-Governor of Bengal, says: "In my judgment, Christian missionaries have done more real and lasting good to the people of India than all other agencies combined."

Turning for a moment to the kindred great Mission field of China, there comes, even as we write, a remarkable "sign of the times," indicative of a great change of policy, if not really of sentiment. Proclamations have been issued, in almost every province, calling on the people not only to live at peace with missionaries and their converts, but also explaining that the Christian religion teaches men to do right, and should

---

[*] See "Independent Testimonies Concerning Missionary Work." Published by the Church Missionary Society.

therefore be respected. The governor of the great province of Chikiang, in which are 12 million people, and the treaty port of Ningpo, tells the people that "the sole object of establishing chapels is to exhort men to do right;" and then follows the wise remark that "those who embrace Christianity do not cease to be Chinese, and both sides should therefore continue to live in peace, and not let mutual jealousies be the cause of strife between them."

In a yet larger province, Kiangsi, the governor tells the people the missionaries have the right to lease ground and houses, and to travel about to preach, "their sole aim being the inculcation of the practice of virtue, and having no design of interfering with the people." Then follows the statement that "such of the subjects of China as wish to become converts may lawfully do so, and as long as they abstain from evil-doing, there is no law prescribing inquisition into, or prohibition of, their action." After threatening punishment on those who destroy chapels and houses, the governor adds: "Bear in mind that when the missionaries live in the midst of your villages, you and they are mutually in the relationship of host and guest." Those in the least acquainted with the past attitude of the government and its great officials towards Christianity, will in all this see remarkable evidence of a changed policy; and the change is a splendid evidence of the leavening influence of Protestant Missions.

Gathering into the briefest possible space the great facts and features of the previous chapters, it will be seen that since the close of last century a remarkable and most encouraging advance in spheres, agencies, and results has taken place.

Then there were but seven Foreign Missionary Societies, and of these four belonged to the last decade of the century. Now the seven have become at least one hundred.

Then the total sum contributed in the year for Foreign Missions was less than £50,000. Now it is £2,250,000.

Then the entire number of missionaries was about 160, of whom 100 were Moravians. Now the number of male missionaries is 3607, and of females, more or less engaged in Mission work, 2322.

Then the number of native preachers was less than 80, and of these not 6 were ordained ministers. Now the number is not far short of 30,000, and of these 2600 are ordained.

Then, throughout all North, East, and Central Africa; Turkey, Persia, and Central Asia; all Northern and Central India, Burmah, Siam, China, and Japan; New Zealand, New Guinea, and Madagascar; the hundreds of islands in the Indian Archipelago and Polynesia—with ten or twelve exceptions—and South America, there were no Protestant Missions. Now, as we have seen, they are found almost among all nations.

Then, in most of those vast regions, there was not a single Christian convert, and in others there were very few. Now we can tell of converts in hundreds of islands, in scores of tribes, from every caste and nationality of our splendid Indian Empire, and in almost every country where the attempt to propagate the faith has been fairly tried; and although in most places the number of converts is small, yet in many countries they are not only increasing, but that, too, at an accelerated speed year by year, and in some regions can be counted by thousands, tens of thousands, and even hundreds of thousands.

Then the Bible was found in about 36 languages, spoken by less than one-fifth of our race, and with a circulation of not more than 5,000,000 copies. Now the whole, or the most important parts, have been translated into 267 languages and dialects, spoken by five-sixths of our race, and with a circulation of not less than 150,000,000 copies.

Then the darkness which had rested for hundreds of years over the Pagan world was hardly penetrated by a ray of

Christian light. Now in some 4000 definite centres the light is placed, and is penetrating all around.

Then Mohammedanism, Buddhism, Hinduism, and the gross polytheisms of Africa and the island world of Asia, were strong and unchallenged in their isolation. Now they are sensibly weakened, and the Christian conception of God, of Christ, of the soul, of sin and of morals, are taught and more or less believed, where formerly they were not known.

Then slavery, polygamy, infanticide, human sacrifices, and numerous customs tending to the degradation of women, were common, and had had almost unchallenged sway for many generations. Now they have been greatly diminished, and are clearly among the things that are evidently passing away.

All these are facts which make it absurd to speak of Missions as a failure. During the past ninety years, Christianity has spread more widely and gained more triumphs than during any period three times as long, since the close of the third century, and Christian Missions have had the largest share in winning those splendid triumphs of goodness, righteousness, truth, and love.

CHAPTER XI.

THE SOURCES AND CULTIVATION OF THE MISSIONARY SPIRIT.

ISSIONS have strong claims on the aid and sympathy of philanthropists, merchants, and statesmen; on all, indeed, who are interested in human progress. They further the legitimate aims and the highest aspirations of such classes. They aim at the repression of every form of cruelty and wrong. Their success always creates or develops trade and commerce. Good government and peaceful aspirations follow where they prevail, and their triumph is as surely followed by a rapid growth of civilisation, as spring is by warmth and fruitfulness. The principles which underlie Missions necessarily lead in these directions, and their history offers a continuous series of facts illustrative of human progress in the repression of evil, and the growth of true civilisation.

It is surprising therefore, and only to be explained on the ground of want of acquaintance with the facts, that the classes in question, unless imbued with the Christian spirit, regard Missions with indifference or prejudice. It is religious people only who originate and sustain Missions with any vigour. Obviously great resources of faith, hope, love, and zeal are required, as well as of money; and the former are found among Evangelical Christians to a greater degree than elsewhere. It is a fact, illustrated in every age of the Church of Christ, that where apostolic, pietist, or evangelical views, as they have been variously named, have prevailed, missionary ardour has been inflamed, and where these have died down or been absent, the missionary spirit has declined. In the few instances in which it has been otherwise, the exception admits of explanation; but the fact, and the rule, cause all deeply interested in Missions, to be anxious for the conservation and spread of this earnest, spiritual form of Christianity, and to view with apprehension any essential deviation from it.

Even when it is recognised, the missionary spirit is not as prevalent and powerful as it should be. We joyfully hail its fuller diffusion throughout Protestant Christendom, with all the liberality it evokes and the agencies, both at home and abroad, that it sustains; and we are persuaded that the cause is a growing and not a declining one. But, when we think of the empires, kingdoms, and tribes still Pagan; of more than one thousand million souls outside all forms of Christianity, the vast majority of whom have never once had the great truths of the Gospel respecting God and Christ, and sin and salvation, presented to them; and when, on the other hand, we think of the immense resources of the Church of Christ, in men, and wealth, and influence; of her freedom from any such stress and strain as have in past ages taxed the energies and absorbed the resources of the true servants of God, and the marvellous facilities now afforded of preaching the Gospel to every creature; the truth is forced on our minds that the want is not so much in the means as in the will to enter on this work, stupendous as it is, in a fitting manner.

Three things are requisite. Two of these constitute our part, the third is with God; and if we fulfilled ours, which are after all only true features of the genuine ideal Christian character, the third would be given. These are—

I. A true conception of the work which is yet needing to be accomplished.

II. Wise, strenuous, and adequate endeavours to accomplish that work.

III. The outpouring of the Spirit of God to give effect to human endeavours.

Here we have sketched the outlines of such a book on the philosophy of Missions as is greatly wanted. Only a partial contribution to so noble a subject can now be given.

I. Christians, generally, utterly fail in forming a conception alike of the magnitude and the importance of the aims contemplated by the missionary enterprise. No one indeed can adequately comprehend what it signifies; but through want of imagination, knowledge, thought, and sympathy with the mind and purposes of God, our conceptions are far lower and weaker than they should be.

Who, for instance, understands, or even tries to understand, what the attempt to convert a million, or a hundred million, or a thousand million Pagans involves; or to understand what is meant by the evangelisation of Central Africa, or New Guinea, or India, or China! How few have any adequate idea, or feeling, relative to the ignorance of all heathen races of essential religious truth, of the crimes and sufferings engendered by this heathenism, or of the vice and immorality prevalent among them.

How few Christians even seem to understand what a misfortune, or calamity, or loss, it must be to be a heathen, and to be without the beliefs and hopes which irradiate our own lives and destinies. How few sympathise with what must be the thought of God, as He surveys the dishonour done to Himself, and the evils inflicted on mankind, by the prevalence of heathenism and its attendant crimes and vices; or the purposes of love and beneficence which the Saviour cherishes toward our race, and which He died and reigns to accomplish. How few, again, in their comfortable and even selfish enjoyment of Christian ordinances, and in their efforts to give the Gospel to those who, with rare exceptions, have had it offered to them, and have turned from it a hundred, nay a thousand times, think of the multitudes of the heathen who are perishing with hunger whilst they have bread enough and to spare. Our selfish neglect of those most needing our aid, and the fallacy of one of our excuses for neglect,—that we have heathen enough at our doors to absorb our efforts,—is forcibly and admirably put in the following extract. Will the reader give it the attention it merits?

"Among the members of the various sections into which the Evangelical Protestant Church in America is divided, there are at the present time labouring in word and doctrine, no less than 78,853 ordained ministers. In the fifteen principal denominations of Great Britain and Ireland there are 39,746 more, making a total of 118,599 ministers set apart, who are, week by week, preaching Christ to a small section of the human family constituting not one-twentieth part of the whole—say seventy millions, out of the world's population of more than fourteen hundred millions.

"On the other hand, these countries have 2900 ordained missionaries witnessing for Christ in heathendom. So that in these two countries there are considerably more than a hundred thousand ministers engaged in instructing seventy millions of intelligent, educated Protestant Christians, while they send less than three thousand missionaries to evangelise the rest of the world, including the thousand millions of heathendom! To reduce the numbers so as to make this state of things more conceivable, a hundred ministers are set to teach seventy thousand Christians, and three missionaries are sent to instruct a thousand thousand utter heathen— a whole million of Pagans!

"But the case is really far worse. America has, in addition to these ordained ministers, 35,000 local preachers, and probably quite as many more lay-agents of other kinds, including Sunday-school teachers; and England has, at the lowest computation, as many more. The total number of Christian labourers in the home field in these two countries, it would be hard in these days to estimate, so numerous are the volunteer forces. Three hundred thousand Christian workers, however, is far nearer the fact than one; while if we count not only the lay-agents, but the female missionaries in heathendom, the total is only 4,533. The proportion of Christian workers absorbed by the home field is therefore more than 99 per cent. Not one out of a hundred of the ministers and lay-workers of the Christian Church is labouring in heathendom, though it contains ten times more souls than Protestant Christendom, and though it is in such an unspeakably needy condition! Two groups are before us. Seventy fat and well-fed people in the one, and a thousand starving creatures in the other. To the former we give a fine batch of large loaves, and to the latter we accord one crumb to divide between them. Do then those who know the Gospel perfectly well already, whether they obey it or not, need instructing or evangelising a thousand times more than those who have never even heard of God or Christ? Ought the agency available for the world's evangelisation to be thus unequally distributed? Are the Protestants of England and America so dark and ignorant that they really require more than 90 per cent. of the preachers of the truth for their own enlightenment and salvation? Is it the genius of Christianity to look every man on his own things, and forget the interests of others? In the natural world some roll in luxury, while others die of starvation; but can it be pleasing to God that the bread of life should be thus unfairly distributed—God, who would have all men to be saved, and come to a knowledge of the truth?

"And the tardiness of the Church in sending her fishers to launch forth into the deep, and let down their nets for a draught, is all the more strange when we note how much better Mission work pays—to use a familiar word—than the ministry at home."* It is clear evidence of this that, whilst

---

* "The Wide World and our Work in it." By Mrs. Grattan Guinness. Hodder & Stoughton.

the average increase of members throughout the Protestant Churches of the United States was last year but 3·10 per cent., in the Foreign Mission Churches it was 7·75. The average Mission contributions of the former was only 32 cents—one shilling and fourpence. But if the sums contributed be apportioned among the attendants on public worship, or the adult Protestant population, the average amount is not half this small amount.

If in any adequate degree we realised the state of the world, and what the Church of Christ is giving and doing for its conversion, surely the measure of our zeal and liberality would be immensely augmented.

II. How are appropriate thoughts, purposes, and resolves to be more generally formed in Christians? They will come wherever the Spirit of God comes in power. But there are certain means which, if conducted wisely, vigorously, and devoutly, will receive the blessing of God. Let me indicate at least some of these. They relate—

1st. To Missionary Societies.

2nd. To churches and individuals at home.

3rd. To Missionaries and individuals abroad.

1st. Where the missionary spirit is deep and true, agents, money, and whatever is requisite for the vigorous prosecution of the enterprise, will be given. But it is not generally so strong as to be independent of much care for its nurture. Too often it is so sensitive as to be easily depressed, and therefore it is of the first importance that all associated with the management of Societies sustain and strengthen the missionary spirit where it already exists, develop it where it is not, yet ought to be, and avoid whatever would create prejudice, which is only too ready to spring into being. Are not the following suggestions important? and it would be but too easy to give abundant evidence that the want of thought, or courtesy, or good sense, or a careless or proud indifference, if not contempt for the opinions of the outside world, has brought much detriment to the good cause, and given its detractors, and even its friends, but too much occasion to withhold from it their support :—

1. The affairs of a Society should be conducted with the most rigid economy; and this should be seen in home management as well as in foreign affairs.

2. It should provide or encourage the production of literature, suited to the young, the intelligent, and the general mass of Christian people.

3. Care should be taken that the pecuniary features of the Society do not prevail over its spiritual aims—that the desire to manage its affairs on "sound business principles" does not cause the diminution of religious fervour and enthusiasm, which after all is its life and soul.

4. Care, too, should be taken that regulations and rules do not strangle free, fresh, and spiritual impulse and movement. A Mission Board has to administer affairs, perhaps in countries as diverse as China and Kaffraria; among races varied as Hindus and Fingoes; in states of society as extreme as those of Japan and Patagonia; and among races as far apart and unsympathetic as Arab Mohammedans, Mahratta Hindus, Siamese Buddhists, and New Guinea fetish worshippers. It has to select men for these various spheres; to co-operate with them in their general work, and in the very peculiar circumstances into which they may be thrown. It has to reinforce their number, to supply them with the means of prosecuting their enterprise in very various directions, and generally to advise them as to the policy they should adopt, and the methods they should pursue. Clearly all this, and a great deal more, requires much wisdom, experience, sympathy, considerable respect and deference for the opinions and wishes of those on the spot, and an elasticity of administration which, judging from the history of many Missionary Societies, has been by no means common.

5. Missionaries should be very carefully selected. Their

spheres should be as carefully chosen. A due amount of freedom should be accorded to them, and especially to those of proved temper and ability, and to such as are in new or peculiar spheres. And respect and honour should be accorded, not only to the office of a missionary, but to every one who is or has been a missionary, if they have borne themselves even fairly and honourably well in the good fight.

6. All associated in administering the affairs of a Society need ever to remember that they are trustees only, representatives of the Christian community appointed for a special purpose, the friends and fellow-helpers of the men who do the actual work, not their superiors and masters; and that the popularity of a Society, the enlargement or diminution of its funds, and the happiness and efficiency of its agents abroad, depends greatly on their wisdom, impartiality, courtesy, and Christ-like zeal.

7. Organisation is important, and, perhaps, expresses better than any other word what should be aimed at in the conduct of a Society. But it should be organising for purposes beyond merely collecting money. It should see to the formation of new auxiliaries, the best arrangement of annual services, the circulation of literature, the appointment of suitable collectors, and the cultivation generally of confidence, enthusiasm, and devotion toward the sacred cause. Next to the one or two secretaries of a Society, ministers, carefully selected, can most efficiently and economically do this around their own spheres.

2nd. Christian Societies, however organised, may well be urged to give Foreign Missions a very high place in their aims. Their place in relation to other objects we will not attempt further to define, than to say it is second to none. If Sunday schools, mission halls, and Home Missions, to say nothing of other wise and holy agencies, can claim a large share in the zeal and liberality of Churches, surely Foreign Missions can claim a larger. Their field of action is most vast and varied, and it is given up to unspeakable ignorance, vice, crime, and misery. It is helpless and hopeless in itself. Yet it is also the most remunerative and reproductive in converts, agents, and pecuniary resources. It is not unreasonable, then, to ask that it have a far higher place in the thoughts, prayers, energies, and gifts of almost every Church than it now has. Instead of this, is it not, in most Christian Societies, feebly supported, little heard of, and soon set aside? May we offer an ideal of what is fitting to represent Missions in every Church?

1. A missionary committee appointed by those in authority, and made as nearly as possible representative.

Its work should be definite, and inclusive of such details as the following—

The cultivation of the missionary spirit.
The diffusion of missionary information.
The collection of missionary funds.
The arrangement for missionary services.

2. A monthly missionary prayer meeting, at which a brief address should be given, to direct the prayers offered to a devout and intelligent appreciation of the missionary problem, and to special cases where prayer may bring the blessing most needed. Pains also should be taken that the meeting may be made stimulative of prayer for the same great objects through the month.

3. A minister may well be expected frequently to refer, in public prayer and in preaching, to missionary topics. But at least once a-year missionary services should be held.

4. A missionary anniversary should be held in every place of worship; and it should be made much of by adequate advertisement and notice, by private invitation, by the presence of neighbouring ministers, and, wherever practicable, by more than one service. A week-night sermon, a breakfast, a tea, a meeting for ladies, a service for the young, or a lecture, may well be added to what is usually called the public meeting. Whenever practicable the services of a mis-

sionary should be secured, but if not, a meeting should still be held. The importance of the enterprise demands this, and it would be a grave reflection on the intelligence and zeal of any minister if, on a subject so vast, varied, and interesting, he could not, with a very moderate expenditure of time, prepare an address which for half-an-hour or more should interest and inform any kind of audience. Sermons that are missionary in either their principles or facts, and not merely in name, should be preached, and whilst at a meeting the missionary should have the larger measure of time, it adds to its importance and interest if both laymen and ministers take a part in the proceedings.

5. At least one collector should be appointed, who, from social position and age, will give weight and authority to all applications for subscriptions and donations. If others are appointed to collect smaller subscriptions, weekly, monthly, and quarterly, to suit the convenience of donors, equal regard should be paid to suitability, punctuality, and reliability.

6. Care should be taken, by circulars and announcements, to foster a true idea of the importance of mission services. The majority of those even who attend places of worship form their estimate of the relative importance of an object from the manner in which it is announced, by ministers and office-bearers. Too often, such announcements are as brief, bare, and cold as it is possible to make them. The missionary anniversary should be certainly the second, if not the first, event in the annual history of every Church, and should be treated accordingly.

7. Endeavours should be made to interest Sabbath-school scholars and others in this enterprise.

(*a.*) A box should belong to each class, and be handed round once each Sabbath.

(*b.*) The lessons now and then should be of a missionary character.

(c.) Some missionary magazine should be circulated as widely as possible.

(d.) A missionary address should be given at least once a quarter.

(e.) Once a year the whole service should be missionary—i.e., the school should have its missionary meeting as well as the congregation.

The importance of these suggestions will be endorsed by all really acquainted with the history of Missions and the biographies of missionaries. A very large proportion of the latter, and the best home helpers, come out of schools where Foreign Missions are made prominent.

8. Every Christian family, and every person claiming to be a Christian, may reasonably be expected to take an interest in Missions. Our ideal of how that interest should be shown, is—

(a.) A missionary box in every house, which, beside being privately used, should be placed on the table once a week.

(b.) A subscription weekly, quarterly, or annually, from every professing Christian.

(c.) A missionary magazine in every family.

3rd. Missionaries, more than any class of persons, elevate or depress the missionary spirit in the Church of Christ.

They are responsible for methods of evangelisation, and for the public opinion of Christianity, as a religion and a life, that is gradually formed in their spheres of labour. They gather the converts, and are to them what shepherds are to sheep. They affect the degree to which native Christian communities become strong, self-reliant, self-supporting and aggressive. They select and train all native agency. They disburse the funds of the Society which they represent. The influential Europeans, who as traders, merchants, travellers, and civil servants, are found in almost all Pagan lands, derive their ideas of Missions from a close, and too frequently unfriendly, observation of missionaries themselves. The letters, reports, and books which missionaries write, and the addresses they deliver, when at home, shape public opinion, not only respecting themselves but of the cause they represent. How much the interest, the ardour, and the liberality of a Christian Society depends for a whole year, nay for many years, on a sermon or an address at a missionary anniversary! Who can measure or describe the widespread and abiding influence of an Egede, a Schwartz, a Carey, a Williams, and a Moffat? Such men are greatly wanted now. Never were so many, wide, open, and promising spheres of labour ready for men of the highest ability, in the various directions of genius, eloquence, and zeal!

But splendid work awaits the willinghood of men less richly endowed. Two classes of such may be indicated—the wealthy and the enterprising.

There are a few—some associated with Societies, others not—who give gratuitous service; a noble example, worthy of wider imitation, and calculated to tell powerfully, not only in favour of Missions, but Christianity itself, both at home and abroad.

Respect and confidence are due to the general policy of our Missionary Societies; but through them, or as entirely independent agents, it would be interesting to see a large class of free, self-denying missionaries, acting somewhat on the methods of the New Testament evangelists, or the Mohammedan missionaries in Africa, of whom we hear so much and know so little. We do not forget that both these classes have moved among races with whom they have had affinities, such as no European or American can have among Asiatics or Africans, and that in some cases the attempt would prove unwise and disastrous. But since some Missions are conducted with elaborate and burdensome expensiveness, it would be an interesting experiment to see other methods tried that were more economical, primitive, and direct. African and Asiatic converts might, in many cases ought, thus to act, for the method is quite in harmony with native precedents; but converts are not likely thus to act, unless stimulated by European example.

III. But apart from methods, that which is wanted is men of power, full of the Spirit of God. Should we not pray that God would make such men? One such in Central Africa, in Japan, China, Burmah, or one of our splendid Indian provinces, might turn the current of popular thought and sympathy in favour of Christianity. This is no mere dream. Oriental gregariousness justifies the thought. Events are preparing for such a revolution of religion; and if Sidharta-Sackya Muni in India, Confucius in China, Choitunya in Bengal, Mohammed in Arabia, and Luther in Germany, profoundly affected the beliefs of millions even whilst they lived, and have permanently formed the religious thoughts and feelings of vast empires, nations, and tribes, it is surely within the reach of probability that some one proclaiming the true message of God in the method of St. Paul, and with the love and power of the Saviour of mankind, may be honoured to produce revolutions as widespread, but far more important and blessed.

The great need—that which would give whatever is lacking—is the power of the Spirit of God, as it was promised by Christ, as it may be had by holy living and ardent desire, and as it has influenced a few here and there. This would make all Churches possessing it intensely missionary in spirit and aim; would constrain the gift of whatever wealth was required, and lead far more to offer their services than could even be accepted. This would elevate and direct the motives and aims of all who received this power from on high; would indefinitely add to the wisdom, love, and energy of Mission Boards; would go out to create in pagan minds a desire for something higher, better, truer than their superstitions, and awaken an eagerness to welcome the Gospel when it was offered to them. This would give power to increase a thousand-fold the converts to Christianity, and would make them individually, as zealous, as holy, and as Christ-like, as were Apollos, Aquila, Priscilla, and Polycarp, and our Churches as pure as those at Philippi and Philadelphia. Then the highest flights of prophecy shall be realised, and the wilderness be turned into a fruitful field, and the fruitful field be counted a forest,—Isa. xxxii. 15-20; xxxv.

> "Come, blessed Lord, bid every shore
>   And answering island sing
> The praises of Thy royal name,
>   And own Thee as their king;
> Bid the whole earth, responsive now
>   To the bright world above,
> Break forth in rapturous strains of joy,
>   In memory of Thy love.
>
> "O come with all Thy quickening power,
>   With one awakening smile,
> And bid the serpent's trail no more
>   Thy beauteous realms defile.
> Thine was the Cross with all its fruit
>   Of grace and peace divine;
> Be Thine the Crown of Glory now,
>   The palm of victory Thine."

TABLE OF BRITISH MISSIONARY SOCIETIES.

When Founded.	Name of Society.	Income for 1886-87.
1701	Society for Propagation of the Gospel in Foreign Parts,	£119,475*
1732	Moravian Missionary Society,	19,037
1792	Baptist Missionary Society,	69,252
1795	London Missionary Society,	105,382
1799	Church Missionary Society,	234,639
1814	Wesleyan Missionary Society,	135,259
1817	General Baptist Missionary Society,	6,949
1829	Church of Scotland Missionary Society,	28,806
1840	Irish Presbyterian Foreign Missionary Society,	9,833
1840	Welsh Calvinistic Methodist Missionary Society,	5,886
1843	Free Church of Scotland Missionary Society,	48,775
	Primitive Methodist Missionary Society,	1,541
1844	South American Missionary Society,	11,848
1847	United Presbyterian Church of Scotland Missionary Society,	38,895

* This, and the incomes of some of the Methodist Societies, are for Continental and Colonial, as well as Pagan Missions.

TABLE OF BRITISH MISSIONARY SOCIETIES—*Continued.*

When Founded.	Name of Society.	Income for 1886-87.
1855	Presbyterian Church of England Missionary Society,	£18,637
1856	Turkish Missions Aid Society,	1,578
1856	United Methodist Free Church Missionary Society,	16,612
1860	Methodist New Connexion Missionary Society,	3,200
	The Universities' Mission (Central Africa),	14,438
1867	Friends' Foreign Missionary Association,	10,516
	China Inland Mission,	18,940
1870	Missionary Leaves Association,	8,816
1871	Original Secession Church of Scotland Missionary Society,	662
1877	Cambridge Brotherhood (Delhi),	656
1881	Oxford Brotherhood (Calcutta),	......
	Kabyle Mission to North Africa,	1,000
1885	Bible Christian Missionary Society,	676
	The Salvation Army,	

TABLE OF SUBSIDIARY BRITISH MISSIONARY AGENCIES.

When Founded.	Name of Society.	Income from Subscriptions.*
1698	Society for Promoting Christian Knowledge,	£52,489
1799	Religious Tract Society,	17,866
1804	British and Foreign Bible Society,	132,771
1831	Trinitarian Bible Society,	2,377
1840	Bible Translation Society,	2,102
1841	Edinburgh Medical Missionary Society,	3,971
1858	Christian Vernacular Educational Society,	5,466
1861	National Bible Society of Scotland,	18,563
1878	Medical Missionary Association,	......

* A part only of these amounts appropriated to Foreign Missions.

LADIES' MISSIONARY SOCIETIES—BRITISH.

Date of formation.	Name of Society.	Lady Missionaries.	Income 1886-87.
1834	Society for Promoting Female Education in the East,	40	£7,382
1852	Indian Female Normal School Society,	30	11,365
1853	Lebanon Schools Society,	...	1,377
1857	Female Education Society, Free Church of Scotland,	30	6,856
1857	Female Association of the Established Church of Scotland,	27	6,357
1859	Ladies' Auxiliary to the Wesleyan Missionary Society,	29	7,922
1860	British-Syrian Schools Society,	...	5,130
1865	Ladies' Association for Promoting Female Education among the Heathen,	...	*6,392
1870	Baptist Zenana Work and Bible Women Society,	44	6,422
1874	Woman's Association, Irish Presbyterian,	6	2,552
1875	London Missionary Society Committee for Female Missions,	24	4,604
1879	Woman's Missionary Association, English Presbyterian,	9	2,715
1880	Church of England Zenana Missionary Society,	87	21,688
1880	Zenana Association U.P. Church of Scotland,	16	4,535

* Included in Propagation Society's accounts.

LADIES' MISSIONARY SOCIETIES—AMERICAN.

Date of Formation.	Name of Society.	Lady Missionaries.	Income for 1886-87.
1861	Woman's Union Missionary Society,	53	£6,947
1870	Society of the Presbyterian Church,	119	25,943
1870	Society of the Presbyterian Church, North-West,	60	13,411
1872	Society of the Presbyterian Church, Northern, New York,	6	2,359
1870	Woman's Board of Foreign Missions, New York,	13	10,027
1877	Woman's Board of Foreign Missions, South-West,	9	1,134
1877	Board of the Presbyterian Church, South,		3,790
1884	Reformed Presbyterians,		
1875	General Missionary Society of the United Presbyterian Church,	12	9,279
1879	Reformed Dutch Church,		3,013
1868	Cumberland Presbyterians,	5	1,355
1869	Board of Missions (Congregational),	98	21,301
1875	Board of the Interior (Congregational),	45	8,753
1871	Board of the Pacific (Congregational),	4	826
1870	Board of the Pacific Islands (Congregational),	1	197
1871	Baptist Foreign Missionary Society,	29	12,956
	Baptist Foreign Missionary Society of the West,	21	5,575

LADIES' MISSIONARY SOCIETIES—AMERICAN—Continued.

Date of Formation.	Name of Society.	Lady Missionaries.	Income for 1886-87.
1873	Free Baptist Foreign Missionary Society,	8	£1,317
1872	Auxiliary to the Board of Missions (Episcopal),	...	4,748
1869	Society of the Methodist Episcopal Church,	68	33,358
1878	Society of the Methodist Episcopal Church, South,	23	9,619
1879	Society of the Methodist Protestant Church,	3	658
1875	Association United Brethren,	7	2,336
1875	Disciple Church, Woman's Board,	3	3,656
1884	Woman's Missionary Society, Evangelical Association,	...	363
1879	Woman's Society, Lutheran General Synod,	7	1,487
1876	Woman's Society, Presbyterian Church, Canada,	...	3,716
1881	Methodist Church in Canada,	4	2,288
1877	Baptist Foreign Missionary Society, Ontario,	3	779
1876	Baptist Foreign Missionary Society, Quebec,	...	......
1881	Woman's Foreign Missionary Society of Friends,	12	2,763

Some of the Societies named are auxiliary and contributory to others, and therefore have no separate agents.

The number of European and American ladies does not always indicate the proportion of native agents employed, or the zenanas or schools in charge, or the number of pupils taught. The agencies employed vary considerably.

ROMAN CATHOLIC FOREIGN MISSIONS.

It is difficult to obtain any reliable information relative to Roman Catholic Foreign Missions, but the following statements are believed to be substantially correct. It is interesting to compare them with Protestant contributions for the same purpose:—

Total European Roman Catholic contributions to Foreign Missions for 1885-6, . . . £265,170

British contributions to the Society for the Propagation of the Faith—

England,	£1,259
Ireland,	3,430
Scotland,	334
	£5,203

St. Joseph's Foreign Missionary Society and College, Hendon, ... 1,665

Total British, . £6,868

DIAGRAM
SHOWING THE POPULATION OF THE WORLD.
Each Square represents One Million of Souls.

HEATHEN	MOHAMMEDANS	JEWS	ROMAN CATHOLICS	GREEKS	PROTESTANTS
833 MILLIONS.	185 MILLIONS.	7 MILLIONS.	190 MILLIONS.	85 MILLIONS.	130 MILLIONS.

TOTAL POPULATION OF THE WORLD, 1430 MILLIONS.

There are about 100 Missionary Societies, with a total of 3600 Missionaries, endeavouring to evangelise the Heathen World. As the direct result of their labours, they can point to two and a-half millions of Native Converts. Let God be praised for these. But think of only 3600 to preach the Gospel to a bewildering total of 1,025,000,000!

DIAGRAM

Showing the chief items of the Annual Expenditure of the United Kingdom for the Ten Years ending 1882, contrasted with the Annual Contributions for Foreign Missionary Work during the same period.

INTOXICATING LIQUORS	£136,000,000
BREAD	£70,000,000
BUTTER AND CHEESE	£35,000,000
MILK	£30,000,000
SUGAR	£25,000,000
TEA, COFFEE, AND COCOA	£20,000,000
COAL FOR HOUSEHOLD PURPOSES	£15,000,000
RENT OF HOUSES	£70,000,000
RENT OF FARMS	£60,000,000
WOOLLEN GOODS	£46,000,000
COTTON GOODS	£14,000,000
EDUCATION	£11,000,000
LINEN GOODS	£8,000,000
CHRISTIAN MISSIONS	£1,050,000

INDEX.

A

Abyssinia, 96.
Africa, Central, 83.
Africa, East, 92, 136.
Africa, Northern, 80, 136.
Africa, South, 70, 90, 136, 147.
Alaska, 132.
Algeria, 82.
America, 50, 136, 167.
America, South, 129.
—— Board of Commissioners, 50, 89, 92, 101, 102, 126.
—— Episcopal Church, 54, 55.
—— Missionary Societies, 50-59.
—— Presbyterian Missions, 87-101.
Aneitium, 126.
Ansgarius Union, 73.
Anstey, Miss, 74.
Annam, 112.
Anniversaries, Missionary, 172.
Arabia, 103.
Armenia, 103.
Arnot, Mr., 93.
Asia, 100, 136.
Asia, Central, 105.
Asiatic Russia, 100.
Australia, 70, 121.

B

Badley, Rev. B. W., 159.
Bahamas, 132.
Baldeus, 30.
Baptist Missionary Society, 38, 86, 88, 106, 131.
Baptist Missionary Union (American), 52, 106, 109.
Baptist Societies in India, 106.
Basel Missionary Society, 64, 72, 107.
Basim Mission, 74.
Benguela, 89.
Berlin Missionary Society, 64, 72, 91.
Bethel Santal Mission, 74.
Bible Society, British and Foreign, 42.
Bible Translation Society, 162.
Board of Commissioners Foreign Missions, 50.
Brainerd, D., 34.
Bray, Dr. T., 35.
Brazil, Christian Union, 74.
Brecklum, Missionary Society, 67.
British North America, 133.
British National Expenditure, and Christian Missions, 186.
Buddhism, 4, 137, 139.
Burmah, 109, 147.

C

Calabar, 85.
Cambridge Brotherhood, 107.

Cambodia, 112.
Cameroons, 85.
Calvin, 29.
Canadian Missionary Societies, 53, 70, 106.
Canadian Missions, 70.
Caroline Islands, 124.
Celebes, 119, 147.
Central Africa, 83.
Ceylon, 30, 110, 147.
Central Asia, 104.
Chicago Training College, 48.
China, 113, 147, 149, 160.
China Inland Mission, 49, 71.
Chrischona (St.) Missionary Society, 67, 97.
Christian Knowledge Society, 35, 131.
Christian Vernacular Educational Society, 42.
Church Missionary Society, 41, 83, 85, 94, 102, 104, 107, 133.
Coillard, M., 92.
Coligny, Admiral, 29.
Colonial Missionary Societies, 42, 47.
Collectors, Mission, 173.
Confucianists, 6, 137.
Congo, 87.
Congregational Societies in India, 107.
Constantinople, 101.
Continental Missionary Societies, 72.
Corea, 115.
Crashaw, W., 33.
Crowther, Bishop, 85.

D

Danish Missionary Society, 68, 73.
Disciples of Christ Missionary Society, 53.
Dorchester, Dr., 76.

Dufferin, Lady, 48.
Dutch Missions, 62, 92, 117.
Dutch Reformed Missionary Society, 72.

E

Early British Missions, 33-36.
Early European Missions, 29, 32.
East African Society, 67.
Edinburgh Medical Missionary Society, 47.
Edinburgh Missionary Society, 41.
Egede, Hans, 31.
Egypt, 81.
Eliot, John, 34.
Ellice Islands, 123.
Ellichpoor Mission, 74.
Episcopal Church Missions, 54.
Ermelo Missionary Society, 62, 72.
European Missionary Societies, 60.

F

Falconer, Keith, 44, 105.
False Religion, 5, 8, 12.
Female Medical Association, 48.
Fernando Po, 87.
Fiji, 124, 147.
Finnish Missionary Society, 69, 73.
Fitzroy, Captain, 129.
Formosa, 115.
France, 68.
Francke, Dr. A. H., 32.
Free Church of Scotland, 43, 91, 93.
Free Will Baptist Missionary Society, 53, 106.
Frere, Sir B., 159.
Friends' Missionary Society, 47, 57, 71, 98, 108.

G

Gaboon River, 87.
Gallas, 96.

Gardiner, Captain A., 130.
Geddie, Dr., 126.
General Baptist Missionary Society, 45, 106.
Geneva Evangelical Society, 68.
German Missionary Societies, 63.
Ghazipur, 74.
Gilbert Island, 123.
Glasgow Missionary Society, 41.
Gold Coast, 84.
Gopalgunge, 74.
Gordon, Sir A., 125.
Gossner's Missionary Society, 65, 72.
Greek Church, 3, 137.
Greenland, 31, 134.
Grotius, 29.
Grundemann, Dr., 75.
Guiana, 130.
Guinness, Grattan, 49, 71, 168.
Gustavas Vasa, 29.

H

Hainan, Island of, 116.
Halle, 32.
Hannington, Bishop, 94.
Harvey Islands, 128.
Hermannsberg Missionary Society, 66, 73, 92.
Hindus, 105, 137.
Hinduism, 5.
Honduras, 130.
Huntingdon's, Countess of, Mission, 47.

I

Independent Missions, 48, 74, 108.
India, 105, 147, 148.
Indian Archipelago, 117.
Irish Presbyterian Mission, 45.

J

Japan, 116.
Java, 62, 72.

Jews, 37.
Joppa (Jaffna), 74.
Judaism, 6.

K

Kabylia, 82.
Kaffraria, 91.
Kaiserswerth Deaconesses, 67.
Kelley, W. W., 74.
Kesub Chunder Sen, 160.
Knacks Missionary Union, 67.
Krapf, Dr., 96.

L

Labrador, 134.
Lagos, 84.
Laos, 112.
Lawes, Rev. W. G., 120.
Lebanon, 102.
Legge, Dr., 149.
Leibnitz, 31.
Leipsic Missionary Society, 66, 73.
Liberia, 84.
Livingstone, Dr., 87.
Livingstone Inland Mission, 87.
London Missionary Society, 39, 90, 95, 97, 113, 120, 122.
Loyalty Islands, 123.
Lunds Missionary Society, 69, 73.
Lutheran Missionary Society, 66.
Lutheran Societies in India, 107.
Lutken, Dr., 32.

M

Macfarlane, Dr., 120.
Mackenzie, Bishop, 93.
Madagascar, 97, 147.
Manchuria, 114.
Marquesas Islands, 124.
Marshall Islands, 124.
Mauritius, 97.

Max Müller, 139, 160.
Mayhew family, 34.
Medical Missions, 47.
Melanesia, 127.
Mennonites, 63, 72.
Methodist Episcopal Church Missions, 53, 54.
Methodist Societies, 54, 107.
Micronesia, 126.
Ministers, 143.
Missionary Review, 148.
Missionary spirit, 164.
Modern Missions, 37.
Mohammedanism, 3, 137, 139.
Mongolia, 114.
Moravians, 31, 61, 72, 90.
Moritz, J. 29.
Morrison, Dr., 114.
Morocco, 82.
Mosquito Coast, 130.
Mumford, Mrs., 74.

N

Netherlands Missionary Society, 62, 72.
Netherlands Union, 72.
New Britain, 121.
New Caledonia, 127.
New Guinea, 120.
New Hebrides, 125.
New Ireland, 121.
New Zealand, 121.
Niger, River, 85.
North German Missionary Society, 66, 72.
Norwegian Missionary Society, 69, 73, 98.
Nyassa, Lake, 93.

O

Organisation, 170.
Oxford Brotherford, 107.

P

Palestine, 102.
Paris Missionary Society, 68, 73, 91.
Parseeism, 6.
Pascadore Islands, 115.
Patagonia, 129.
Persia, 103.
Phillipine Islands, 120.
Philosophy of Missions, 20.
Pilgrim Fathers, 34.
Pilgrim Society, 73.
Plutscho, H., 32.
Polynesia, 122.
Preparatory work, 145.
Presbyterian Church of England, 45.
Presbyterian Societies in India, 107.
Presbyterian Mission Board (American), 55, 101, 107, 114.
Propagation Society, 35, 46, 92, 99, 131.
Protestantism, 1, 137.

R

Raleigh, Sir W., 33.
Religions of the World, 137.
Religious Tract Society, 42.
Results of Missions, 138.
Rhenish Missionary Society, 65, 72, 91, 119, 121.
Robert College, Constantinople, 101.
Roman Catholicism, 2, 137.
Roman Empire, 40.
Roman Missions, 5, 181.

S

Salvation Army, 50, 108.
Samoa, 122, 147.
Sandwich Islands, 51, 124, 147.
Sargent, Bishop, 150.

Schleswig Missionary Society, 67, 73.
Scotland, Church of, Missionary Society, 43, 93.
Selwyn, Bishop, 127.
Sen, Kesub Chunder, 160.
Seventeenth Century Missions, 29.
Seventh Day Baptists, 53.
Seychelles, 97.
Shintoism, 6, 137.
Siam, 111.
Sierra Leone, 83.
Society Islands, 123.
Soudan, 83.
South American Missionary Society, 129.
South Australian Missionary Society, 106.
Southern Baptist Convention, 53.
South Seas, 122, 136.
Spirit of God, power of, the great need, 176.
Stockholm Missionary Society, 69, 73.
Sunday Schools, 173.
Sungaria, 114.
Swedish Missionary Society, 69.
Swedish National League, 69.
Switzerland, 68.

T

Tahiti, 122.
Tanganyika, Lake, 95.
Taoists, 137.
Taylor, Bishop, 50, 74, 88.
Thibet, 114.
Thompson, Sir Rivers, 160.
Tierra del Fuego, 129.
Tinnevelly, 150.
Tokelan Islands, 123.
Tonga, 124.

Tract Society, 12.
Tripoli, 82.
Turkey, 100.

U

Uganda, 94.
United Presbyterian, 44, 86, 91.
United States, 132.
United States Expenditure and Christian Missions, 77-79.
University's Mission, 93, 97.

V

Vanderkemp, Dr., 40, 90.
Vaud, Canton de, Society, 68, 73, 92.

W

Walleus, 29.
Warneck, Dr., 135.
Welsh Calvinistic Methodists, 45.
Weltz, Baron Von, 31.
Wesleyan Missionary Society, 42, 84, 91.
West Indies, 130, 147.
Whateley, Miss, 74, 81.
Women's Missions, 47, 180.
Women's Union, German, 67.
Women's Societies, 180.
World, population of, 1.

Y

Yeretsian, Dr. A., 102.
Yomba Country, 85.

Z

Zambesi, 92.
Zanzibar, 97.
Zeist Missionary Society, 72.
Zenana Medical College, 47.
Ziegenbalg, B., 32.
Zinzendorf, Count, 31.

www.ingramcontent.com/pod-product-compliance
Lightning Source LLC
Chambersburg PA
CBHW020926230426
43666CB00008B/1581